MY DECLARATION
A CHALLENGE FOR MEN TO **RISE-UP**

JEFF MANESS

LG

Lauren Grant
Publishing & Design

Published in 2018 by Lauren Grant Publishing

Any Internet addresses, company or product information printed in this book are offered as a resource and are not intended in any way to be or to imply an endorsement by Lauren Grant Publishing, nor does Laurent Grant Publishing vouch or the existence, content, or services of these sites, companies or products beyond the life of this book.

Unless otherwise noted, Scripture quotations are taken from *Holy Bible,* New Living Translation, copyright © 1996, 2004, 2007, 2013, 2015 by Tyndale House Foundation. Used by permission of Tyndale House Publishers Inc., Carol Stream, Illinois 60188. All rights reserved.

Scripture quotations marked NIV are from the *Holy Bible, New International Version*®. NIV®. Copyright© 1973, 1978, 1984 by International Bible Society. Used by permission of Zondervan. All rights reserved worldwide.

ISBN 978-0-692-16892-9

Library of Congress Control Number: 2018910610

Cover design by Brielle Lidtka
Author photo by Rugged Grace Photography

Printed in the United States by Morris Publishing®
3212 East Highway 30
Kearney, NE 68847
1-800-650-7888

TABLE OF CONTENTS

FOREWORD

Most Christian men I meet, do not actually act like they know the King of Kings.

Many Christian men will tell you they have "accepted Jesus" into their lives but their actions (how they actually live their life holistically and fully) is counter and quite mediocre to what they believe.

A One-dimensional Man

Many men can and do accelerate in one area of their life only. They are rather one-dimensional. They are great with their business or profession - but they are fat. They are great with their faith - but ignore their wife and kids. They are super healthy and look like a Greek god - but they are jerks. They are great with their kids and are super intentional - but they have zero communication with their God.

Across the four areas of a man's life (1) God, (2) wife and kids, (3) profession or business, & (4) body ... men focus on one area and neglect the other three. You know this is true because you have seen this in other men. At best, you may meet occasionally, a two-dimensional man.

You see, I believe that God is the King of Kings. I believe that his Son, Jesus died on the cross and was raised to life three days later (all of which Jesus predicted). I believe this with my whole being and this belief brings me power. Power from the King of Kings ... directly to me. So, if God is my King of Kings, and Jesus saved me, then I am His child. Which makes me a King.

Are *you* a King?

Do you live your life in such a way that you have been entrusted with something? I do. I see *all* that the King of Kings has entrusted to me as my kingdom to steward. A kingdom, where every morning I report to the King of Kings on how I am doing, how I am acting, and how I am expanding. A kingdom where I am accountable for my relationship with God and we communicate. A kingdom where I grow in my connection to my wife and kids. A kingdom where I accelerate my business. A kingdom where I acknowledge that God chose my body to do the work to support the other areas of my life. A kingdom where I am expected to expand ... because expanding is leading a life that is abundant.

Show me a Christian man who stewards his life well across all four areas and I will show you a man (a king to the King of Kings) getting it done. He's doing the work. He's not waiting on anyone. He's expanding the kingdom and producing results across his whole life, not just one area.

Abundance = Expansion

In John 10:10 (NIV), Jesus said, "I have come that they might have life, *and* that they might have it abundantly." Spend any amount of time reflecting on the word "abundant" you'll quickly come to the word "expansion." Jesus is calling us to expand in all four areas of our lives. To be men who *do* and *act* like they are kings to the King of Kings.

I have now known of Jeff Maness for close to ten years. As I have had the privilege to walk with Jeff over that time, I have witnessed a Godly, Christian man who is four-dimensional. Not only have I seen Jeff's belief manifested in action ... I have also witnessed a man who knows his King of Kings. His faith is important ... but don't miss this ... Jeff acts on his faith. He does the work, daily. He gets after it ... each and every day.

I am proud to call Jeff my Brother. And, I am equally proud of this book and its possible impact in your life. I hope this book challenges you like never before. I hope this book disturbs you to *act* and *do* the work. I hope this book prompts you to get after all four areas of your life. I hope you start to see that the King of Kings is calling you to expand like never before.

Do the work.
Read this book.
1 - 2 - 3 off you go!

> **-Bryan Miles**
> CEO & Co-Founder of <u>BELAY</u>

ACKNOWLEDGEMENTS

Jesus, without You I am nothing. The longer I live, the more that becomes a reality for me. Thank You for saving me, sanctifying me with Your Spirit, and setting me free to live for You. May my life reflect Your goodness and Your glory. This is my declaration!

Sabrina, you are my biggest fan. I love that! You are always encouraging me to do the next thing or go on the next adventure, and that includes this book. Thank you for walking beside me wherever God leads. I couldn't ask for a better partner in life. I love you.

Jonah, Mariah, Makalah, and Jaydah, you are my pride and joy. I pray that I can model for you the words that make up the message of this book. You four are my "why". I believe in you, I love you, and I will stand with you no matter what comes your way.

Dad, this is a book for men and I couldn't ask for a better man to lead me than you. Thank you for leading the way, and modeling for me a heart that is fully devoted to Jesus. Mom, thank you for putting up with dad and I! Your prayers, support, encouragement and commitment to the call of God for our family is unmatched. I love you both.

Todd, you are a friend I didn't even know I needed until you came into my life. You are my armor bearer, confidant, encourager, prayer warrior, and "the king's friend". I have grown so much in what it means to be a man because of you. Thank you for being my Hushai. I want to be like Todd when I grow up. I love you.

For all the men who have chosen to rise-up in my life and boldly live out your faith in Jesus, thank you. The list would be far too long to mention here, but I am the man I am today because you were the men you were called to be. I pray that I might influence other men the way you have influenced me.

Betsy, your commitment, dedication, and hard work on this book are incredible. My Declaration would not be a book without your involvement. Thank you for all you do to make my vision become a reality. You are a blessing.

THE WHY

To my son Jonah, any future son-in-laws, and grandson(s) - You are my "why" for writing this book. I pray over us the same thing King David challenged his son Solomon with:

1 Kings 2:1-2 As the time of King David's death approached, he gave this charge to his son Solomon:[2] "I am going where everyone on earth must someday go. Take courage and be a man. [3] Observe the requirements of the Lord your God, and follow all his ways. Keep the decrees, commands, regulations, and laws written in the Law of Moses so that you will be successful in all you do and wherever you go."

1 Chronicles 28:9-10 [9] "And Solomon, my son, learn to know the God of your ancestors intimately. Worship and serve him with your whole heart and a willing mind. For the Lord sees every heart and knows every plan and thought. If you seek him, you will find him. But if you forsake him, he will reject you forever. [10] So take this seriously."

There is nothing I desire more for you, and nothing I want to model better than this - to "take courage and be a man", and to take God and our faith seriously.

You have a heritage that is firmly rooted in Jesus. For generations in our family, there have been men who rose-up from their greatest failures to live with great faith. I want you to know that my love for you, and God's love for you, is not based on what you do. We love you for *who* you are.

To Jonah: You are my son. That can't be taken away. I believe in you. I'm proud of you. I know you have the strength, in Jesus, to do what He's called you to do and be who He's called you to be. I will walk beside you, stand with you, and fight for you to the very end. I've prayed for you since before you were born, that you would be as "bold as lions" (Proverbs 28:1) in your faith. You are gifted, compassionate, full of life, and are a natural born leader. As God molds those things into His image you will be unstoppable on His behalf. I can't wait to see what He does through you.

To my daughters: While this book isn't written directly to you as women, it is written to the men who will be influential in your life. As I write this book, I'm not just thinking about the kind of men I want us to become, but the kind of men I pray will become your husbands. Marriage may not be a part of God's plan for each of you, but if it is, the kind of man I pray God brings you is found in the pages of this book. Don't settle for anything less than God's best. You each deserve that.

To any future son-in-laws: If the Lord wills for my daughters to marry, you will be His appointed leaders for them and the shepherds to any grand-children He provides. I've prayed for you daily, before I ever knew your names. I've prayed for your faith, your purity, your values, and your commitment to my daughters and your children. You are an answer to my Genesis 24:50-51 prayer! I know that on your wedding day I will be able to truly say, "Here is my daughter, take her and go. May she be your wife as the Lord has directed." I'm expecting you to lead the way in submission by seeking, serving, and spoiling them; loving them as Jesus has loved you! (You better, because I know where you live!)

To any future grandsons: One of my prayers is that I would get to know every one of my grandchildren. Yes, I pray that prayer because I want to hold you in my lap, play games with you, read you books, wrestle with you, and watch you learn to navigate life. That's not the heart of my prayer though. I want to know you, so I have a chance to pass on my faith to you as my grandparents did for me.

I had amazing grandparents. I knew they loved me, but more than anything, I knew their love for me was rooted in their love for Jesus. I wish you could have known them. I only pray that you are still impacted by their lives through my influence on yours.

To each of you: As we go where everyone on earth must go someday, may we take courage and be men. May our declaration be that we will finish what God started in us by being aggressive at purity, taking responsibility, honoring God financially, living for eternity, leading courageously, and leaving a legacy. We can't do this alone. We need each other. That's what you'll find in this book. It starts today. I love you all.

This is my declaration!

From Dad, Jeff & Grandpa

INTRODUCTION

There is a beautiful diversity among men today that doesn't get celebrated enough, so thankfully not every man will fit the following mold: For the most part, even in our diversity, men are simple! Someone once said, "Men only need three things in life and they all start with 'S' - sleep, steak, and sex; air is optional."

What can I say? For most of us, we're simple. This doesn't mean we're stupid or shallow, just simple. So, to help everyone out, let me explain.

Most of us can only do one thing at a time. Whatever we *are* doing we are fully engaged, but we can only do one thing. That's why if we're watching the game or a movie, playing video games, or involved in some other activity, we may not respond - even when you repeatedly say our names. It's not that we don't want to talk to you, it's that we don't even know you're talking to us. I tell my wife and kids all the time, "Unless I acknowledge that you've said my name, I have no idea you're talking to me." Once you have our attention, we'll be fully engaged with you. We're just simple.

We need direct. Not directions, that's another subject, we need direct. We don't pick up on signals, we cannot decipher relationship riddles, and if you don't clearly state it we will never just figure it out. We do want to know what you're thinking, but we won't, unless you tell us. Hints don't help either. We're just simple.

Outside of the men that God has uniquely gifted with creativity, we typically don't care what color the kitchen is or what palette is used in the bedroom. For more information on what we think about the kitchen and bedroom go back to the three "S's". We're just simple.

And speaking of colors, we tend to see primary colors only. Red, yellow, blue, and the colors they make - green, purple, and orange.

Fawn is a baby dear. Mango is a fruit. Mint is something we want in our ice cream. Almond is a nut. Champagne and coffee are drinks. Charcoal is what we grill with, and russet is a potato loaded with cheese, sour cream, and bacon.

Chocolate or rose are gifts. Mahogany is the wood our bed is made of, midnight is what happens while we sleep on that bed, sunrise happens after we sleep, and zinnwaldite brown? We don't know what the crap that is! (It's a real color. I looked it up.)

Not all men enjoy sports but for those of us who do, the only other colors we know are tied to our favorite teams: Crimson and Crème. Brown and Gold. Maze and Blue. We're just simple.

We live deeply, love passionately, and learn quickly. We long to be accepted, we crave encouragement, we need respect, and we desperately want someone to believe in us. Our potential is unlimited, our personalities broad, our interests varied, and our talents vast.

Hollywood has done a great job of making men in the relationship appear to be the bumbling idiot who is the brunt of all the jokes. At times, the Church has done a masterful job of pointing out what we suck at instead of praising us for where we're strong.

So, men, here's the thing - because we're mostly simple I'll get straight to the point. I don't know where you come from, I don't care who you are, and it doesn't matter what you've done. This book is more than just revealing our weaknesses, it's about rising-up to live in our strengths.

Young and old, single or married, all colors of skin, Christian or not, God has wired us as men in a unique way. He has wired us just the way He wants us. We might be simple, but we are strong! So, let me speak to that strength.

We have each experienced pain, so what if we allowed a purpose to be birthed out of that pain? We want to be bold, so what if we became bold in our faith? We can be aggressive, so what if we became aggressive at purity? We've been given authority, so what if we took responsibility for that authority and used it to build others up instead of tear them down? The world around us is driven by money, so what if we honored God financially? We are meant to live for something bigger than ourselves, so what if we started living each day as if eternity hangs in the balance? We are designed to lead, so what if we led courageously? We love a great story, so what if we left a legacy with our lives?

It's time to rise-up men. It's time to rise-up and be the kind of men this world needs. Not men in quantity but men in character.

This book is written for men, and with men in mind. As a man, I tend to believe I'm familiar with what we believe, how we feel, and the way we operate. I know that's a broad statement and there are obvious exceptions, but for the most part, men are men.

> IT'S TIME TO RISE-UP AND BE THE KIND OF MEN THIS WORLD NEEDS.

While our experiences are unique, our interests varied, our personalities vast, and our talents broad, our life is lived out through a similar framework. That doesn't mean a woman shouldn't read this book or can't get anything out of it, I just want to be up front about its purpose.

I actually hope that through this book God ignites a new passion in the hearts of women to see the men in their lives live out God's calling. I pray there will be wives who see their husbands in a new way. Moms who pray for their sons with new fervor. Sisters who stand beside their brothers with a new-found commitment. I pray this book will raise-up a new generation of warrior women who will fight *for* the men in their lives and not just *with* them! I pray for a revelation from God that leads to a revolution for God.

As men, I truly believe that when we live out our God given potential in this world, everyone benefits. When we lead in our purpose we enable others to live in theirs as well. When we love as we are called to love, we allow others to experience God's love as they were designed. When we serve because of God, it opens other hearts to seek the God who first served us.

This is not about our power as men, but it is about our position. Not a position of dominance over others, but one of dependence upon God and on each other. Dependence is hard for us. We believe we can figure it out, fix it on our own, or find another way, but we aren't made to stand alone. We aren't meant to fly solo. We desperately need God, and we definitely need each other!

"My Declaration" is a series of statements designed to lead us to a place of surrender. A surrender to God and a surrender from self. We are typically "doers" as men, but our doing must be born out of our being…who we are and most importantly, Whose we are.

This book does not contain all the answers and it definitely won't provide a quick fix for all our problems. What it will offer are some principles for life, that if lived out, can lead us to the place we long to be.

I can't make these choices for you and I can't force you to rise-up. So, this is *my* declaration and I'm challenging you to make it *yours* as well. I don't know all of you, but I believe in every one of you. I know it won't be easy, but I can promise you it will be the best.

Starting today, may we rise-up to be all we are created to be. Starting today, may we be men.

This is my declaration!

ONE

FINISH WHAT WAS STARTED

As a man, I can't finish what was started in me unless I surrender every part of me.

The key to a great kiss is a good start, but if you don't finish well, you're doomed. It's a double-edged sword. Do you remember your first kiss? (If you're married and your wife is reading this with you, the only kisses you remember are with her. *wink wink*) I don't remember every kiss in my life, but there is no way I'll ever forget my first, and it's not because of how great it was either.

I was 16 years old and had been dating my very first girlfriend for several months. Neither of us had shared a kiss with anyone before so I had been plotting our first kiss for days. When was the right time? Where was the right place? How do you start that initial move? What if she doesn't move back? Just thinking about it made my palms sweat. This was a big deal.

For some reason, my twin brother was with my girlfriend and I as we went out that night. I don't remember if there was a fourth person previously, but by the time we were dropping her off at her house it was my brother, my girlfriend, and me. We pulled up to her home and being the gentlemen that I was (plus I was planning on my first kiss), I walked her to the door.

We stood on her front porch for what seemed like an eternity. We talked about the evening, held hands, and stared into each other's eyes. The time was just right. It was now or never. I remember thinking, "If you don't kiss her now, you will never kiss anyone in your life." It's a tad over dramatic, but I was a 16-year-old male! What do you expect? So, I did it! During a lull in our conversation I took the plunge.

Since I always saw people in the movies close their eyes when they kiss, I closed my eyes, pursed my lips, leaned in, and planted one on my girlfriend. The moment was…not what I expected. What I felt on my lips could only be described as, not another pair of lips, but I smooched anyway, pulled back, only to realize the horror of what I had just done.

In that split-second lull in our conversation, while I had decided to lean in with my eyes closed and plant the best first kiss this world had ever seen, she decided to break the awkward silence by saying something. In what can only be described as divine or deadly timing, my lips met her mouth as she was opening it to speak, thus causing me to surprise her with a kiss on her pearly white teeth. I was mortified.

I opened my eyes to the realization that our first kiss would be one where our lips didn't even touch. This couldn't get any worse. "What do I do?" I thought. Logic would have said, apologize, make light of the moment and say, "Let's try that again." But logic was long gone at this point. My life was over, right? How would we ever recover? I could have just finished what I started, but in the panic of the moment, I put my head down in shame and walked back to the car.

My brother, who had been pretending not to watch from the vehicle, was eagerly waiting for a report. I got into the car and heard, "So, how did it go?" "Just drive, man" I said. "Just drive!" What started out with great intentions, ended in settling for a long and disappointing ride home.

Settling is where a lot of us men have found ourselves in our lives. Have you ever started something with great intentions, like my kiss, but it didn't end up the way you expected? Starting something is easy, right? It's the finishing that makes us strong. That's why it's time to rise-up! It's time to rise-up and finish what was started in us.

Something was started within us when we were born, and that something still remains. It might be lying dormant waiting to rise. You might believe it's dead, but you don't realize it can be brought back to life. It may be your life's greatest disappointment, but that doesn't mean it can't become your greatest comeback story. Men, it's time to rise-up!

It's time to rise-up and be the kind of husbands our wives seek, the fathers our children need, the sons we are called to be, the men on whom our friends can lean, and the leaders this world desperately needs. The reality is, no matter who you are, what you've done, or where you've been, God started something in each of us when we were born and it's time to finish what He started.

There are men who gave God a chance at some point in their life but have since walked away, or simply stopped walking at all. It's time to rise-up!

There are marriages that started out great, but the years have worn you down, both sides have made mistakes, the situation has changed, and the relationship is hanging on by a thread. It's time to rise-up!

There are dads who, when your kids were little you were all in, but as they have gotten older and you got busier, the relationship has grown distant and you think to yourself, "If I could only go back and do it all over again." It's time to rise-up!

Or maybe you're a man and your dad was never there. He wasn't involved in your life, or if he was, it wasn't a positive experience. You just want to finish what he meant to start or could have started in your life, but never did. It's time to rise-up!

Or perhaps you're like me and your dad was there. He was your hero. He did lead by example. He invested in your life and you're thinking, "How could I ever live up to the level my dad started?" It's time to rise-up!

For some men, everything is great for you right now. You're living for Jesus; your relationships are healthy and strong, and you just want to be sure that you don't mess this thing up. You aren't in a season of defeat or discouragement, you're just willing to do whatever it takes to rise-up and finish what was started in you.

Whatever the case, whoever you are, and wherever you've been, I believe God has birthed something within us as men, and I want us to finish well. We can't go back and fix what has happened, but we can rise-up and finish what was started. So how do we do that? How do we finish what was started in us?

There's a story in Genesis 11 and 12 that I have read dozens of times. Each time I read through it, I knew it was a part of a greater story, I just never saw it connected to a part of my story. Then one day as I was reading through it again, God allowed me to see it in a whole new light.

Genesis 11:31 [31] One day...

I love the phrase, "One day" in the Bible. I know it's only two words, but they are two very powerful words. The phrase "One day" is used one hundred and twenty times in Scripture to start a sentence. At times, it is not so good.

"One day the serpent came to Eve..." or, "One day, Cain suggested to his brother..." Or, "One day, Noah drank wine, got drunk and lay naked in his tent." (Someone's thinking, "That sounds like an old college story of mine.")

Then there are other "One day's" in the Bible that stand out. "One day, Moses was tending the flock of His father in law, Jethro." It was on that day that God led Moses to Mount Sinai where he received the calling to lead the people of Israel out of their slavery in Egypt.

"One day, Jesse said to David, 'Take this basket of food out to the battle field and see how your brothers are doing." Which, by the way, this "One day" led to the slaying of Goliath and the deliverance of Israel from the Philistines.

Time and time again in the stories of Jesus, you see the phrase "One day". One day Jesus was teaching on a hillside, walking on the shore, or going to the temple. It was on those days that the dead were raised to life, the blind receive their sight, the ears of the deaf were opened, destinies changed, lives transformed, sins forgiven; and all of it happened on "One day".

I say all that, to say today could be *your* "One day!" You might believe it's just another day. If you were writing your own story you might say, "One day, I decided to read this book." But this day could be the "One day" your life changes forever.

Today could be the day God gives you a calling for your life or slays a giant in your life. Today could be the day God forgives yours sins, fills you with His Spirit, restores a relationship, or heals a disease. Whatever it is, today could be your "One day."

In one day, Jesus can do for us what we can't do for ourselves in an entire lifetime. He doesn't even need one day. All it takes is one moment and He can change your life forever. This could be that moment. This could be your "One day."

Genesis 11:31 **³¹ One day Terah took his son Abram (Abraham), his daughter-in-law Sarai (Sarah), and his grandson Lot and moved away from Ur of the Chaldeans. He was headed for the land of Canaan, but they stopped at Haran and settled there.**

I think there is more to the word "settled" here than just "that's where they made their home." The plan was to make it to Caanan but they settled to live in Haran. This is the set up for everything else in the story we are reading, and this explains a lot of our story as well. God wrecked my heart with that one word. "Settled."

THERE IS TOO MUCH SETTLING GOING ON IN OUR MANHOOD TODAY.

There is too much settling going on in our manhood today. We were headed on a God sized mission, but we settled for mediocrity. We were headed for purity, but we settled for pleasure. We were headed for a bold faith, but we settled on blending in. We were headed for courageous leadership, but we settled for a cowardly life. We were headed for a healthy marriage, pursuit of a call, financial freedom, raising our kids, restoring our relationships, and the list goes on, but we settled.

Oh, how I pray that God unsettles us as men today. As men, we aren't meant to settle, we are meant to soar. Terah was headed for Caanan, but he settled for Haran.

Genesis 11:32 [32] **Terah lived for 205 years and died while still in Haran.**

Men, don't miss this. If we don't move on from where we've settled, we will die there as well. Settling never leads to life. It always leads to death.

Why did Terah settle in Haran? Did you know that Terah had a son named Haran? Haran was the brother of Abram, but he died while they lived in Ur. Is that why Terah settled? Was the pain of his past too much to bear so he settled? Did he name the place of his settling after his greatest pain? I don't know. I don't know why Terah settled, but I do know that in this place where he settled, God was about to finish what was started in Abram.

Genesis 12:1-9 [1] **The LORD had said to Abram, "Leave your native country, your relatives, and your father's family, and go to the land that I will show you.** [2] **I will make you into a great nation. I will bless you and make you famous, and you will be a blessing to others.** [3] **I will bless those who bless you and curse those who treat you with contempt. All the families on earth will be blessed through you."** [4] **So Abram departed as the LORD had instructed, and Lot went with him. Abram was seventy-five years old when he left Haran.** [5] **He took his wife, Sarai, his nephew Lot, and all his wealth—his livestock and all the people he had taken into his household at Haran—and headed for the land of Canaan. When they arrived in Canaan,** [6] **Abram traveled through the land as far as Shechem. There he set up camp beside the oak of Moreh. At that time, the area was inhabited**

by Canaanites. [7] Then the LORD appeared to Abram and said, "I will give this land to your descendants." And Abram built an altar there and dedicated it to the LORD, who had appeared to him. [8] After that, Abram traveled south and set up camp in the hill country, with Bethel to the west and Ai to the east. There he built another altar and dedicated it to the LORD, and he worshiped the LORD. [9] Then Abram continued traveling south by stages toward the Negev.

It is here that God rocked my world with this passage. Are you ready for it? Abram lived out with *his* life, what his father had intended to live out for his own. Abram finished what was started.

There have been too many generations of well-intentioned men who desired to get to Canaan, but settled for Haran instead, and they died there. So, the settling stops here men! Mediocrity stops here. Addictions stop here. Broken marriages stop here. Financial messes stop here. Absent fathers stop here. It has to!

I don't want to get to the end of my life, look in the eyes of my son or the men of the next generation and say, "Well, I hope you can do better." I pray that we set the bar so high and accomplish so much that we are able to say to the next generations, "Look at what Jesus is *able* to do! Now, you take it to a whole new level!"

So, how do we finish what was started in us? I believe Abram finished what his father started because he lived out four specific principles in his life, and if we want to finish what was started in us, we need to do the same. First, I need to hear what God says about me.

God told Abram, "Leave the land your dad settled for and go to the land I will show you." He didn't even tell him where he was going first, he was just following God in faith. Why would Abram blindly follow God? Why would he just finish what was started? Yes, I think Abram wanted to obey, but I also believe Abram heard what God said.

Right after telling Abram to "go," God told him what He would do through Him, including: I will make you into a great nation. I will bless you. I will make you famous. You will be a blessing to others. All the families of the earth will be blessed through you.

Do you know what I hear when I read all that? "You were made for more than Haran. Your dad might have settled there but I will take you to Caanan. This is who you are." Abram acted on what God spoke to him because he heard what God said about him.

> ABRAM ACTED ON WHAT GOD SPOKE TO HIM BECAUSE HE HEARD WHAT GOD SAID ABOUT HIM.

Do you know what God says about you?

Ephesians 2:10 [10] **For we are God's masterpiece. He has created us anew in Christ Jesus, so we can do the good things he planned for us long ago.**

You are a masterpiece, not a mistake. Just because you made mistakes does not make you a mistake. Just because you failed does not make you a failure. Your parents may not have planned to have you, but that doesn't mean you don't have a purpose or a plan for your life. No matter what anyone has told you and no matter how you've been made to feel, you are a masterpiece in the eyes of God!

But it gets even better. Not only are you a masterpiece, but you are also made to do good things. Yes, we struggle believing what God says about us, but we also struggle being who God says we can be. You are made to do good things. You're not made to settle in Haran, you are meant to succeed in Canaan.

God is saying to you, "I still believe in you. You're meant for more than this. You're not a lost cause. You haven't committed too many sins. You've not fallen too deep, run so far, or settled so long that I can't redeem you."

You need to hear what God says about you. No matter who you are, what you've done, or how you've been made to feel, you are a masterpiece, and you're made to do good things. That leads right into the next thing Abram did, which we also need to do. I need to do what God tells me to do.

God told Abram to **"go to the land I will show you… So Abram departed as God instructed."** (Genesis 12:1-4) He heard what God said about him, and because he heard, he did. Notice, Abram was 75 years old. I'm not saying that's old, I'm just saying it's never too late for you. If you're still breathing, then God is still birthing a purpose for you in your life.

So, what is God telling you to do? He's speaking to some of you right now. That tug on your heart or pit in your stomach, that's God. He might be asking you to give your life to Him right now. Maybe He's asking you to restore that relationship, rebuild that marriage, or refocus your priorities. Maybe you need to commit to Him financially, invest in your children, or surrender the addiction. Whatever it is and however old you are, you need to hear what He says about you, do what He tells you to do, then you need to give credit where credit is due.

God told Abram, "Leave the land your dad settled in and go to the land I intended for him. And by the way, I believe in you. I will make you famous. I will bless all the nations through you. You are a masterpiece and I made you to do this."

Verse 6 tells us that Abram left and took everything with him when he went. His wife, his wealth, his work, his kids, his house, and his livestock. He took *everything*! Do you know what that says to me? It says that following God requires everything! Following God is an all or nothing proposition. As a man, I can't finish what was started in me unless I surrender every part of me.

> AS A MAN, I CAN'T FINISH WHAT WAS STARTED IN ME UNLESS I SURRENDER EVERY PART OF ME.

So, Abram takes everything with him, arrives in Canaan, and on two different occasions he built an altar, dedicated it to the Lord and worshipped God. In other words, He gave credit where credit was due. Often, especially as men, our attitude is to blame God for all the bad stuff in our life and take credit for all the good.

We say things like, "I'm a self-made man." If you think about it, that's the dumbest thing we could ever say, especially to God. My "self" hasn't made jack. The only thing I made by myself was my own sin, and I'm only able to sin because God gave me the freedom to choose it and then He sent His Only Son to forgive me of the only thing I could accomplish on my own. Sin. So, congratulations to me.

Every good thing we have and everything good thing we've accomplished is only because of God. Any family, health, wealth, or happiness exists because of Him. My next breath, yes that one you just took, is a gift from our Creator. There is no such thing as a self-made man. Whether we acknowledge it or not, we are all God-made men, and the only way we're going to finish what was started is by giving all of the credit to Him. So, "God I'm all Yours! Everything I have is Yours and all I have accomplished is only because of You."

Lastly, after I hear what God says about me, do what He tells me to do, and give credit where credit is due, I need to keep taking ground as long as I need to.

This was so encouraging to me. Notice, it says Abram set up camp in Shechem. He didn't settle there, he just set up camp there. Then it says he traveled south and set up camp in the hill country…but he didn't settle there either. Verse 9 tells us he continued to travel south by stages toward the Negev. Abram never settled where he camped, he just continued taking ground all the way to Canaan.

One of the reasons we settle as men is because we see how far we have to go and how much we still need to change. Haran was 600 miles from Ur, where they started, and Canaan was another 500 miles from there. I'm starting to understand why Terah settled, right?

Imagine, no Siri giving you directions. No leather seated SUV with four-wheel drive and air conditioning. No on-board DVD player to keep the kids occupied. It was 500 miles of walking, or at best, riding camelback through rugged, rocky terrain. They couldn't get to their destination overnight, and we can't either. I know we want to get there by sun up tomorrow, but the only way to get there is by stages today.

Finishing what was started is a process. It's a journey that takes time. In fact, it's a journey that will take all the time we have left in this life. The remainder of this book is about that journey. Don't settle because you can't get there tomorrow, instead, finish what was started by taking ground today. What ground does God want you to take?

I don't know about you, but I didn't start well. While I know I may not have started well, I'm dead sure I want to finish well. I haven't always done right, but I want to finish by doing all I can to make it right. So many times, I've settled, but I'm done settling and I'm going to finish what was started in me.

For all of us, Canaan can seem a long way off, and it is. So how can I finish what was started?

I will hear what God says about me, do what He tells me to do, give credit where credit is due, and keep taking ground as long as I need to. I know that if I'm still breathing, then God is still birthing a purpose in me. He's not done working in me, nor is He done working through me, I just need to focus on the next thing He's asking of me.

This is my declaration!

TWO

My Place Of Pain

Most often, it's from the place of our greatest pain that God will birth our greatest purpose.

Pain is what causes us to settle. Pain is what makes us stop. Whether the pain is too much to bear or feels too great to overcome, we often seem to give up. So, before we can continue with our declaration we first need to deal with our defeat. Before we move ahead in our purpose, we first must deal with our pain.

I believe, without exception, that every man has suffered great pain. It might appear in different forms and rise to different levels, but it is all born from the same places. In that pain is where many of us settle, yet it's out of that pain that God wants to birth our purpose. Most often, it's from the place of our greatest pain that God will birth our greatest purpose.

Personally, I'm writing this book from a place of pain and not one of pleasure. I put off writing this book for several years, believing I wasn't good enough, wasn't ready, or didn't have the right things to say. In fact, it was through a season of pain that God confirmed in me it was time to write.

> MOST OFTEN, IT'S FROM THE PLACE OF OUR GREATEST PAIN THAT GOD WILL BIRTH OUR GREATEST PURPOSE.

Pain always births a purpose. There is no path to success that doesn't require pain. No victory without first experiencing defeat. This is true in lifting weights, learning to ride a bike, finding the love of your life, winning the Super Bowl, or rising to the top of your company. To reach the level we desire in life we must first walk through the pain of defeat. Pain always births a purpose.

In no way am I saying that God always leads us to a place of pain, but I am telling you that He will allow it and leverage it for His purpose. God never allows in our lives what He is not willing to align to His will. He always has a plan to redeem our pain. Like a phoenix that rises from the ashes, so our purpose can rise from our pain.

Some of you are reading this from a place of unimaginable pain. Something was done to you that has never been expressed in words. Something was taken from you that can never return. Something was caused by you that you can never undo.

I don't know why God allows us to experience this pain. I don't have an explanation for the bad thing which happened to you, or why He let it be done by you. I don't believe in a God who causes bad things to happen, but I do believe in a God who has a cause, even in bad things, and you are a part of His cause.

You have a purpose. God has a plan for you! Even from the place of your pain, God has a plan for you. In sharing my pain, I pray it will help you rise-up from yours. While the details may be different, I believe the birth place of our pain is the same. Each of us will have some form of pain from three specific places: our past, our people, and a prodigal (Luke 15:11-32). Here is the story of my pain.

The Pain Of My Past:

As I laid in bed that night, the darkness which enveloped me was almost more than I could bear. It was beyond the physical darkness in the room, it was the spiritual darkness I had allowed to control my life. "What have I done?" I kept asking myself. "How did I let it get this far?" I felt like an absolute failure to God, to my calling, and to my wife. "I can't confess this to her. What will she say? What will she do?"

It was probably only minutes, but it felt like I laid there for hours. I had already come clean to God about my sin and experienced His grace, but through His refining process He had asked me to come clean to my wife. I hadn't told anyone else except God. Telling Him felt like the easy part. I mean, He already knew, right? But, telling my wife? This would crush her. I believed it could destroy our marriage.

I wasn't the man I portrayed myself to be. I wasn't the man she believed me to be. I had lied and manipulated her. I had said I was a "man of God" while seeking to fulfill my "manhood" in ways that completely opposed Him and my vows to her. I didn't have a physical or emotional affair with someone else, but I had been unfaithful to my wife with my eyes and mind.

It started out with "innocent" curiosity, but you know what curiosity does to the cat (Too bad all cats can't suffer that fate, just saying). Like Eve in the Garden, I was lured in by the enemy's lies. "God's keeping something from you! It's not that bad! Did God really say you can't look at that?" I was hooked. Like an ox to the slaughter, I was caught in a pornography trap that I couldn't escape.

If only I had asked for help at the beginning, but I didn't know who to ask. If only I had confessed the first time, but I didn't know what to say. I was embarrassed, ashamed, and afraid. In my shame, the sin grew, and in the darkness so did my despair. I wanted out so badly, but I didn't know how! I wanted help desperately, but I didn't want to admit what I had done.

"I'll never do it again!" I'd say. Only to be right back in it the next day. What I wanted to do I couldn't, and what I didn't want to do I couldn't stop. Then one night, like the one at the start of this story, I couldn't sleep. "When will this ever end?" I thought. "How can I escape?" I felt like God prompted me to get up and read my Bible, so I did.

It was January 20th (2003), so I went to Proverbs 20, and began to read. I came to Proverbs 21:21 which says: **"Whoever pursues righteousness and unfailing love will find life, righteousness, and honor." (NIV)**

I wasn't pursing righteousness or unfailing love. Not even close. No wonder I couldn't experience life, no wonder my heart was full of sin, and no wonder I felt anything but honor. I was pursuing unending lust not unfailing love. The Word cut me to the core. It was like God inspired Solomon to write that verse, so I would read it in that moment on that day for that reason.

On January 21st, 2003, I surrendered that part of my life to God. I had asked for forgiveness before, but this time was different. This was more than forgiveness; it was letting God fill that part of my life with His Spirit! Trust me, the desire didn't go away but my slavery to it did. God did something in me that night I could never do for myself. God set me free.

So, back to my original story. As I laid in the darkness next to my wife, I knew if I was going to never be that man again, I had to tell her about my past. I was forgiven and had been set free, but I was not fully honest with my wife. I didn't just sin against God I had sinned against her and I needed her forgiveness as well.

Finally, I worked up the courage and woke her from her sleep. "Babe, I have to tell you something," and the words poured from my heart. I told her everything. The lies, the deceit, and the betrayal. I told her about what God had done for me, but it didn't stop the pain of what I had done to her. She was silent. I didn't know if this was a good or bad thing, all I knew was it was no longer the thing locked in the darkness. It was out. It was in the light.

I wish I could tell you it was easy after that. I wish I could tell you that our marriage thrived. It didn't. It was days before we spoke, and it was months before I felt we were back to "normal". Although I'm not sure we even knew what a healthy normal was. What I did will never be forgotten, but it was forgiven. God had set me free and He has now redeemed that part of my life into part of His purpose for me.

The pain of what I did to God and my wife has not gone away. I know our marriage is still affected by the wounds of what I have done. The enemy still reminds me of who I used to be. Even in writing this book I've heard his accusing voice. "You can't write about purity; don't you remember what you did? You can't challenge men to rise-up, don't you remember how you fell?"

The pain of what I've done will always remain, but the prison that it held me in is gone. Only through facing that pain head on could I live in God's purpose from here on. What is the pain of your past? Everyone has something. It may be different than mine, and the degree of damage might not be the same, but it still exists. Will you let God use the pain of your past to birth a purpose in your present?

> THE PAIN OF WHAT I'VE DONE WILL ALWAYS REMAIN, BUT THE PRISON THAT IT HELD ME IN IS GONE.

The Pain Of My People:

When I say, "my people," I'm not talking about people who belong to me, but the people who are closest to me. In this case, the people I lead at Element Church. It's because of the pain from my past that I'm so passionate to see men set free from theirs. I've heard it said, "Find out what makes you mad, what makes you sad, and what makes you glad. It's in those three things you'll discover your purpose."

I don't know of anything that saddens me more than men who are trapped in the pain of their past, specifically their past (or present) sin. It's infuriating to me how the enemy seems to win the day. The statistics on pornography, infidelity, failed marriages, broken homes, and fatherless children tick me off more than anything in this life. At the same time, there aren't many things in life that thrill me more than seeing men come alive, experiencing the full life of victory available to them in Christ!

Being the Lead Pastor at Element Church has brought me some of the greatest joy in my life, but also some of the greatest pain. I've seen marriages ripped apart by the ravages of sin. I've seen men who were free from addictions only to be sucked back into the vortex of dependence. I've seen guys come through our doors from prison, longing for a purpose and a place to belong, only to turn back once again to the very thing that put them in prison in the first place. I've heard stories I wish I'd never heard, but I can also tell stories I'll never tire of repeating.

So many men are broken today. So many men are lost. Not all men are this way, please don't hear that. As I said, there are amazing stories of restoration and freedom in our Church as well as around the world, but it seems like for every story of victory we celebrate there are 5 stories of defeat that bring us down.

Right now, my purpose might be birthing from the pain I see in my people, but for some of you, the pain of your people is not something you see in them but something they did to you. Some of you have wounds so deep, caused by people you love, and the thought of filling those gaps in your life seems impossible. The pain of your people is a barrier you can't seem to break, a hurdle you can never seem to conquer, or a chasm you can never seem to cross.

OFTEN, OUR GREATEST BLESSING IS WAITING ON THE OTHER SIDE OF OUR GREATEST BURDEN.

My challenge to you is, don't run from that pain but run to it. Better yet, run through it. Often, our greatest blessing is waiting on the other side of our greatest burden. Yes, it hurts. Yes, it has created ripples in your life that have affected nearly every part of your life. Yes, the memory may never go away, but the mastery over you can. You don't have to be a slave of what was done to you. God wants to take even that part of your life, redeem it, set you free, and use it to ignite a burning passion in you as well. A passion that will set this world ablaze with God's glory!

What pain from your people is God wanting to turn into a passionate purpose for your life? Was there something done to you that God wants to use to work through you? Once again, I don't know what the pain of your people is, but God wants to use it for a purpose that is fully His.

The Pain From A Prodigal (Luke 15:11-32):

Prodigals know the love of God, but they don't care to live in it right now. They're runners. Running from the very thing they know will bring them peace. Searching for fulfillment. Longing for acceptance. The prodigal is trying to fill their life with anything they can find, thinking it will give them life. But it's empty. It's vain. It's fruitless. You either have been a prodigal yourself, you are one now, or you care deeply for someone in your life who is a prodigal.

This was the final straw for me confirming it was time to write this book. It was time to rise-up. You see, I've been the prodigal before too. If I don't watch my life closely and depend on the Holy Spirit every day, I could very easily be one again.

On the flip side, I've felt the embrace of our God who is merciful and compassionate. I've experienced His grace. I've been filled with His love. I know what it's like to have a party thrown on my behalf in Heaven because "the prodigal child has come home."

Since I know what that's like, it pains me even more to watch someone I love walk through it. As I write, there is someone in my life who is living their prodigal story. They may not see themselves as a prodigal yet, but I know what they are headed towards. I know they will feel the shame. I know they will live with the guilt. I know they will tell themselves the same lies, ask the same questions, make the same bargains, run the same scenarios in their mind, and it breaks my heart.

My pain is so great for this prodigal it birthed the purpose for this book. I felt God say, "I want you to write from a place of pain." So here I am. My past, my people, and my prodigal. My pain can cause me to settle, and it has, or it can make me soar. The choice is mine. I choose to soar!

So, that's my story, what's yours? What part of your past is God wanting to use for His purpose? What people have brought pain in your life that God now wants to use to reach more people with His life? Are you the prodigal? Is it time to come home? Do you love a prodigal? Are you waiting for them to come home?

I don't know what your pain is or where it came from, but I know we all have pain. So, let me end this chapter where we started: Most often, it's from the place of our greatest pain that God will birth our greatest purpose. Pain always has a purpose. I'm choosing to live in mine.

This is my declaration!

THREE

BOLD FAITH

A bold faith will rise only when a bold faith is required!

In May of 2013, my wife and I took our daughter Mariah to Elitch Gardens amusement park in Denver, CO for her 10th birthday. Mariah is a lot like me in that she loves amusement parks, especially thrill rides. There is a ride at Elitch's which epitomizes thrill rides called The XLR8R. (Pronounced "accelerator")

The XLR8R is not included in the price of admission to the park, you pay extra to experience this ride, and the moment my daughter saw it she wanted to ride it. It's easy to want to ride it when you're just watching it, and I tried convincing her of that, but it's another thing all together when you really experience the ride.

The XLR8R is described by Elitch's as a mix between skydiving, bungee jumping, hang gliding, and I'll throw in there "near death experience," because that's what we were about to go through. Riders are placed into a full body harness, attached from behind to a steel cable, pulled 150 feet up into the air, suspended on a giant trussing system where you then experience a brief free fall, followed by swinging until you stop or plunge to your certain doom.

The moment Mariah saw it she said, "I wanna do the XLR8R daddy, I wanna do it!" "Are you sure babe?" I asked. "It's easy to see these other people do it. It's a lot different to face it on your own. I'm not sure you really want to do this." But she insisted. She was bound and determined to conquer the XLR8R.

We paid the extra money, signed up, went through the safety briefing, got our harnesses on, and walked out under the trussing system to get hooked up for our tandem jump. We stepped on a scissor lift with two other employees which took us a few feet up in the air. As one employee behind us started hooking our harnesses together and attaching us to the cable, the other was giving us instructions about the ride. They were telling us important things like, "Keep your arms locked together. Don't die." You know, important things like that.

After all the instructions were given and the harnesses were attached to the cable, they dropped the lift just a few inches. Those few inches were all we needed to be completely suspended by the cable, flipped forward, horizontal to the ground. At this point I was ready to get off the ride, but it was all or nothing now. We were going to face this thing.

"When you get up to the top" the employee said, "you'll hear someone over the loudspeaker say, 'Three, two, one, GO!', and you'll need to pull the rip cord on your harness to start your free fall." He may as well have said, "You're both going to die!" because that's how I felt in that moment.

Before we knew it, we were 10 feet off the ground, then 20, then 30. It was then my daughter started saying, "I don't want to go daddy, I don't want to go!" I was like, "Too bad girlfriend. We paid good money to ride this thing, we're already up in the air, so the only way off is to finish this ride." I tried reassuring her with my words saying, "It's gonna be ok. This is safe. They wouldn't let people do it if it wasn't secure. Besides, if we hit the ground we'll die on impact." On the outside I was trying to reassure her, but on the inside, I was also saying, "I don't want to go daddy, I don't want to go!"

We eventually got all the way to the top. 150 feet looks a lot higher when you're looking down instead of looking up. No wonder the people we were watching earlier were screaming the entire time. Then we heard over the loudspeaker, "Three, two, one, GO!"

I pulled the rip-cord, but something wasn't right. Instead of releasing us to glide down attached to the cable, it somehow loosened my daughters vest and she began to fall out. Just before she slipped through I grabbed her arm as she hung there…just kidding. That didn't happen, but it would make for an awesome story.

"Three, two, one, GO!" I pulled the rip-cord and we plunged in an exhilarating free fall. The cable caught us at just the right time and we swung out over the on looking crowd. It was incredible. We even have video evidence to prove it. My daughter and I still talk about it to this day, and I think we might even be willing to do it again.

Here's the truth in this whole story and how it relates to us as men today. For those of us who believe in Christ as Savior, we "say" we want to live a life of faith. Not just a faith that God exists but living out a bold faith. The kind of faith that says, "I exist to do whatever God wants me to do, go wherever He wants me to go, risk whatever He wants me to risk, sacrifice whatever He wants me to sacrifice, and face whatever He allows me to face." We all want a faith, not as bold as one lion, but a faith as bold as lions, right?

Proverbs 28:1 The wicked run away when no one is chasing them but the godly are as bold *as* lions.

This is the kind of faith we see displayed in the Bible. In Hebrews 11, many Christians call this chapter "The Hall of Faith," the writer gives a hall of fame list of Bible names. It begins with Abel, Enoch, Abraham, Sarah, Isaac, Jacob, Joseph, and Moses. Then it records this:

Hebrews 11:32-35a [32] How much more do I need to say? It would take too long to recount the stories of the faith of Gideon, Barak, Samson, Jephthah, David, Samuel, and all the prophets. [33] By faith these people overthrew kingdoms, ruled with justice, and received what God had promised them. They shut the mouths of lions, [34] quenched the flames of fire, and escaped death by the edge of the sword. Their weakness was turned to strength. They became strong in battle and put whole armies to flight. [35] Women received their loved ones back again from death.

I don't know about you, but as someone who believes in God and who wants to live out a bold faith, that fires me up! When I read stories like those I want to storm the gates of hell with nothing but safety goggles and a water pistol. I say, "I want a faith like that!" But do I? Do I really want a faith like that?

Here's the thing. I'm not sure I really do. I think we lie to ourselves a little bit in the Church, or at least misunderstand our faith. We say we want a bold faith, but I'm not sure we fully understand what it means. We say we want to rise-up and finish what was started, to live out our purpose that is birthed through our pain, but do we really know what it's going to take? We say we want to live like the people in Hebrews 11, but we don't think about what is required.

Their faith overthrew kingdoms, right? We love that part, but it means they were required to take on kingdoms in battle. They shut the mouths of lions, which means they were in the depths of the lion's den. They quenched the flames of fire, which means they were thrown into the fiery furnace. They escaped death by the edge of the sword, which means they were placed in dangerous situations. They were strong in battle, which means they were required to fight. They received their loved ones back from the dead, which sounds amazing, but to receive a loved one back from the dead they had to first lose a loved one to death. I mean, we say we want a faith like that, but do we really?

We're all for rising-up to finish what was started, facing our greatest pain, and living out a bold faith until we really see what it requires of us. The same thing I told Mariah about the XLR8R is true about us in our faith. It's one thing to see someone else face trials like those and conquer them, it's another thing altogether to face it ourselves.

One of the reasons we settle, fail to rise-up, or don't ever deal with our pain is because we don't know if we have what it takes to face it. We're not sure we have the kind of faith the people in Hebrews chapter 11 had, so we settle for a less burdensome faith. But the people in Hebrews 11 didn't know they had what it took either. Do you realize that?

The people in Hebrews 11 didn't know they had a kingdom conquering, lion chasing, fire quenching, sword wielding, battle ready, death defying faith either, until they faced it. That's a truth I'm still learning to live in myself, and one we all need to learn if we are going to rise-up and live out a bold faith.

A bold faith will rise only when a bold faith is required.

So where does a bold faith come from? If it rises only when it's required, I want to know what the root of that faith is.

In Daniel chapter 3, we read the story of Shadrach, Meshach, Abednego, and the fiery furnace. This is my favorite Bible story of all time. Most of us probably know a little about the story but let me give you some background in case you don't, or a refresher even if you do.

> **A BOLD FAITH WILL RISE ONLY WHEN A BOLD FAITH IS REQUIRED.**

In the first part of Daniel we learn that the King of Babylon (Modern day Iraq), Nebuchadnezzar, invaded Jerusalem, ransacked it and took the best of the young men and women back to Babylon as slaves. Four of those young men were Daniel, Hananiah, Mishael, and Azaraiah. Those were their Jewish names. The king changed their names to Belteshazzar, Shadrach, Meshach, and Abednego.

Even in the names they were given, the king was trying to force them into submission to his ways and his belief. He was demeaning their faith by demanding they change their names. Belteshazzar means "May Bel protect his life" and was a total slam on their God. In giving Daniel that name, Nebuchadnezzar was announcing, "Your God couldn't protect you, so my god is the only true god."

In fact, all their new names had something to do with the gods of that culture. Some of the meanings are unclear, but many believe that Shadrach meant "Command of Aku" the moon god. Meshach meant "Who is like Aku". Abednego meant "Servant of Nebo", another pagan god. So, in their new names they were being conditioned to look to Bel for protection, look up to and obey Aku, and be servants of Nebo! Keep this in mind for later.

It might sound contradictory, but even in their slavery God blessed these young men because they chose to honor Him with their life. They refused the King's way, choosing the way of God instead, and they began to excel in their physical, mental, and social stature.

Nebuchadnezzar took notice of this, moved them up the ranks of the Babylonian government, eventually placing Shadrach, Meshach, and Abednego in charge of all the affairs of the province, and Daniel became a part of the Kings court. They were all well respected, highly trusted advisors to the king.

In Daniel 3, Nebuchadnezzar made a gold statue that was 90 feet tall and 9 feet wide. He sent messengers across the entire province, commanding everyone everywhere to gather at the statue. The king then gave orders to bow to the ground and worship the statue when you heard the sound of the instruments playing. Anyone refusing to obey the orders of the king would immediately be thrown into a blazing furnace to die.

Daniel 3:7-12 [7] So at the sound of the musical instruments, all the people, whatever their race or nation or language, bowed to the ground and worshiped the gold statue that King Nebuchadnezzar had set up. [8] But some of the astrologers went to the king and informed on the Jews. [9] They said to King Nebuchadnezzar, "Long live the king! [10] You issued a decree requiring all the people to bow down and worship the gold statue when they hear the sound of the musical instruments. [11] That decree also states that those who refuse to obey must be thrown into a blazing furnace. [12] But there are some Jews — Shadrach, Meshach, and Abednego—whom you have put in charge of the province of Babylon. They pay no attention to you, Your Majesty. They refuse to serve your gods and do not worship the gold statue you have set up."

This is huge. I had never noticed this before. I've been exposed to this story my entire life. I've taught on this story dozens of times, but

I never noticed this one truth. This changed the entire story for me, and it has the potential to change our entire life.

The astrologers said to the king, "But there are some *Jews*...", then he gave their *Babylonian* names, "Shadrach, Meshach and Abednego." Their character though wasn't rooted in the names the king gave them, their character was rooted in the names their God had given them. Haaniah, Mishael, and Azariah. Do you want to know what those names mean? This changes everything.

Hananiah means "The Lord is grace or gracious". Mishael means "The Lord is the greatest" or "Who is like the Lord?". Azariah means "The Lord helps". Isn't that amazing?

The names the king gave them were rooted in culture, but the names God had given them were rooted in His character! They weren't standing in the identity the king gave them, they were standing in the identity of their One True King. Their bold faith rose only when a bold faith was required, and their bold faith came from knowing Who they were standing in. They were standing in the Lord.

Men, our identity is not found in how we fit into the culture around us, it's found through our faith in Christ who is in us. It's not in what other people think about us, but what Jesus already said is true for us. It's not about being accepted by a certain crowd, but by already being accepted by Jesus Christ. It's not in what we achieve in this life, but by what has already been achieved for us in the next life.

Hananiah, Mishael, and Azariah knew Who they were standing in, they were standing in the Lord! From their identity rose-up a bold faith, right when they needed it most. They may have been called, "Bel protects. Look up to Aku. Obey Aku. Serve Nebo.", but their identity was "The Lord is gracious, the Lord is the greatest, and the Lord helps us."

"But there are some Jews...", the astrologers said. That's what I'm praying over us! Oh, how I pray it would be said of us, "But there are some men. Young men and old, single or married, who refuse to serve your gods and do not worship the gold statues you have set up!

But there are some men who will rise-up and be bold in their faith for Jesus, who stand in their true identity, able to overcome the pain of their past, the pain of their people, and the pain of the prodigal. But there are some men."

God, we are asking You, in this generation, to raise-up more men who will live in the spirit of Hananiah, Mishael, and Azariah. We are asking You, O God, to enable us to live in this identity: "The Lord is gracious, the Lord is the greatest, and the Lord helps us."

Men, when it comes to how we handle sin in our life. When it comes to how we handle our social, personal, private, businesses, and family life. When it comes to how we live, lead, and love, it's time for us to rise-up and have a bold faith. "But there are some men…"

Wow! What if that was said about the men in your Church? What if that was said about the men in my Church?

A bold faith will rise only when a bold faith is required, and it first rises from knowing Who you're standing in, and we are standing in the Lord!

Daniel 3:13-17 [13] **Then Nebuchadnezzar flew into a rage and ordered that Shadrach, Meshach, and Abednego be brought before him. When they were brought in,** [14] **Nebuchadnezzar said to them, "Is it true, Shadrach, Meshach, and Abednego, that you refuse to serve my gods or to worship the gold statue I have set up?** [15] **I will give you one more chance to bow down and worship the statue I have made when you hear the sound of the musical instruments. But if you refuse, you will be thrown immediately into the blazing furnace. And then what god will be able to rescue you from my power?"** [16] **Shadrach, Meshach, and Abednego replied, "O Nebuchadnezzar, we do not need to defend ourselves before you.** [17] **If we are thrown into the blazing furnace, the God whom we serve is able to save us. He will rescue us from your power, Your Majesty.**

By the way, they didn't know the rest of the story. We read stories like this, and other great Bible stories, as if the characters knew what was going to happen. Shadrach, Meshach, and Abednego had not read ahead. There was nothing yet to read. They didn't go to Sunday School and learn about themselves. They weren't living out some bizarre fantasy, they were living out their bold faith. They didn't know what God was about to do, they just knew what their God was able to do.

Their character had brought them to a crisis in their faith. Would they choose to blend in, to cower in fear, and be comfortable in their faith, or would they choose to rise-up and be courageous? How easy would it have been to just take a knee this one time? God would understand, right? We don't often think about this, but there had to be other Jews there as well. Were these three young men the only ones who rose-up to stand out?

Men, there is coming a day. I don't know when or how it's going to happen, but there is coming a day when being a Christian in America will no longer be accepted. How will we respond when our character brings us to this crisis in our faith? If we're not willing to rise-up now when it may just cost us our comfort, convenience, or reputation, what will we do when it might cost us our life?

This is where the bold faith of Shadrach, Meshach, and Abednego brought them. They knew Who they were standing in which led them to know when they would stand firm. A line had been drawn in the sand. They worked in the kingdom. They were friends with people from the kingdom. They even submitted to the king of this kingdom, until it came time to deny their One True King. That's where they drew the line. That's where they stood firm.

"Throw us in the fire," they said. "Our God is able to save us. We've heard the stories of old. We sat around the dinner table as children and listened to our fathers tell us about Abraham, Isaac, and Jacob. We know the stories of David, Gideon, Samson, Joshua, and Caleb. Our God parted the waters of the Red Sea, so He can certainly protect us from you!"

Daniel 3:18 [18] But even if he doesn't, we want to make it clear to you, Your Majesty, that we will never serve your gods or

worship the gold statue you have set up."

"Even if He doesn't." That's one of my favorite statements in all the Bible. Not only had a line been drawn on when they were willing to stand firm, but a line was also drawn on what they were willing to sacrifice. They were willing to sacrifice their lives.

Here they were, standing before the man who held their lives in his hands. "You might set yourself up as an object of worship oh king, but we worship only one King. Our faith is in Him alone. He is able to save us. He is powerful enough to rescue us. We even believe that He will. But even if He doesn't. Kill us if you want, oh king, it doesn't matter, we already died to ourselves and are living for the King of Kings!"

What happened when they stood strong in the face of the king? The king flew into a rage, ordered the furnace heated seven times hotter than before, bound these young men with ropes, and threw them into the furnace to die. Daniel records the fire was so hot, even the soldiers who threw them in died from exposure to the heat.

For many Christians around the world today, the story ends there. No parting of the waters. No slaying of the giant. No victory parades. I know, anti-climactic, right? But that's just it. The most powerful part of this story is not what God does next. We've made it out to be, but it's not.

In all the great Bible stories we teach, we tend to focus on the physical miracles, and to some degree we should. They are incredible, God honoring events. But the most powerful part of this story is not what God does next, it's what He already did in the hearts of these three young men leading up to this moment.

For all they knew, they were about to die in the flames. Like David who stood before Goliath, willing to perish. Joseph, who ran from Potiphar's wife ready to rot in jail. Joshua, who walked around Jericho prepared to look like a fool. The biggest miracles weren't in what God did around them, it was what God had done within them, and it's about what God can do in you too!

Every great Bible story hero did what they did because they knew Who they were standing in; they were standing in the Lord. Their identity was rooted in the Lord. They knew when they would stand firm, drawing an uncompromising line in the sand. Perhaps most importantly though, they also knew why they were standing strong.

THE BIGGEST MIRACLES WEREN'T IN WHAT GOD DID AROUND THEM, IT WAS WHAT GOD HAD DONE WITHIN THEM, AND IT'S ABOUT WHAT GOD CAN DO IN YOU, TOO!

Shadrach, Meshach, and Abednego were thrown into the fiery furnace. Everyone expected them to burn up in the flames and be made an example of by the king.

Daniel 3:24-30 [24] **But suddenly, Nebuchadnezzar jumped up in amazement and exclaimed to his advisers, "Didn't we tie up three men and throw them into the furnace?" "Yes, Your Majesty, we certainly did," they replied.** [25] **"Look!" Nebuchadnezzar shouted. "I see four men, unbound, walking around in the fire unharmed! And the fourth looks like a god!"** [26] **Then Nebuchadnezzar came as close as he could to the door of the flaming furnace and shouted: "Shadrach, Meshach, and Abednego, servants of the Most High God, come out! Come here!" So Shadrach, Meshach, and Abednego stepped out of the fire.** [27] **Then the high officers, officials, governors, and advisers crowded around them and saw that the fire had not touched them. Not a hair on their heads was singed, and their clothing was not scorched. They didn't even smell of smoke!** [28] **Then Nebuchadnezzar said, "Praise to the God of Shadrach, Meshach, and Abednego! He sent his angel to rescue his servants who trusted in him. They defied the king's command and were willing to die rather than serve or worship any god except their own God.**

This was the 'why' for Shadrach, Meshach, and Abednego. They weren't in this for their own glory, they were in this for the glory, honor, and praise of their God. They wanted more people to worship their God, know their God, and follow their God. This wasn't an, "I don't want to go to hell." motivation. It wasn't a, "better place in the kingdom." motivation. This was a, "bring glory to our God!" motivation, and it needs to be ours as well.

When we rise-up to overcome the pain of our past, people, and prodigal. When we rise-up to unsettle the settled places in our life. When we rise-up to live out the bold faith we are called to live. When we rise-up to face our fears and our foes, it needs to be for one reason alone; the glory, honor, and praise of our God.

Yes, Shadrach, Meshach, and Abednego were given a better place in the kingdom. Yes, they became "famous". But their motivation was never to be famous, it was simply to be faithful to the Famous One (God). What's our motivation? How and why will we live out a bold faith?

John Wesley said this: **"Give me one hundred men* who fear nothing but sin, and desire nothing but God, and I care not a straw whether they be clergymen or laymen; such alone will shake the gates of hell and set up the kingdom of heaven on Earth." - John Wesley**[1] (*original quote used "preachers")

A bold faith will rise only when a bold faith is required. So, I will choose to rise-up and live out my faith by knowing Who I'm standing in; I'm standing in the identity of the Lord! I will know when I'll stand firm; drawing an uncompromising line in the sand. And I'll know why I'm standing strong, I'm standing for the glory, honor, and praise of my God.

This is my declaration!

--- FOUR ---

Aggressive At Purity

The progress you make in your purpose is directly linked to the purity you choose to pursue!

Sex is awesome! How's that to the start off a chapter? It's awesome! It is a gift from God, and I want to be the first to say, "Thank you God for such a wonderful gift." I even feel confident in saying there is a Biblical command for us to have sex. It's a beautiful thing! It can enrich and enhance a relationship. It's one of the keys to intimacy in a marriage. Without a healthy sex life, it can be incredibly damaging to a marriage.

Sex is awesome, beautiful, beneficial, even commanded by God... *within* His design. So, what is God's design? I believe the Bible is clear, God's design for the act of sex is between one man and one woman, within the bond of marriage, for a lifetime. There are other examples of sex in the Bible, but the only positive and affirming examples God gives us to engage in the act of sex is within that design. I know I may have lost some of you already but hang with me.

As men, our wife is the only legitimate place where we can participate in a God honoring sexual relationship. Wives, you need to understand this too. You are the only legitimate, God honoring sexual partner for your husband. We might seek sexual fulfillment in other places, but it is only sanctified by God in our marriage. Everything else is impure.

It's been said that everything rises and falls on leadership[1] (John C. Maxwell), but I believe for men, everything rises and falls on purity. Once we decide to rise-up and finish what was started. Once we acknowledge our pain, set out on a course to overcome it, and pursue a purpose through it. Once we choose to live out a bold faith in our lives, the very first thing we face in our path is our purity, or lack thereof.

IN FACT, THE PROGRESS YOU MAKE IN YOUR PURPOSE IS DIRECTLY LINKED TO THE PURITY YOU CHOOSE TO PURSUE.

Nothing derails the pursuit of God's purpose in our lives more than impurity. You might have an incredible gift of leadership, honor God financially, use your authority properly, be extremely successful in your career, but one act of impurity can bring everything God accomplished in every other area of your life crashing down. In fact, the progress you make in your purpose is directly linked to the purity you choose to pursue.

One act of pleasure can bring down years of development in other areas of our lives. One moment of passion can create mounds of pain, and the devil knows this. He's been playing the same card since the Garden of Eden. The devil has been trying to destroy God's purpose in our lives ever since He created it! Look at the purpose God gave Adam in the beginning.

Genesis 2:15 [15] The LORD God placed the man in the Garden of Eden to tend and watch over it.

In essence, God was saying to Adam, "This is your purpose. I spoke this masterpiece of a world into existence and I'm charging you with its care. This is the highest of all honors. I trust you, I believe in you, and you were made for this!"

Genesis 2:16-17 [16] But the LORD God warned him, "You may freely eat the fruit of every tree in the garden—[17] except the tree of the knowledge of good and evil. If you eat its fruit, you are sure to die."

We don't know how many trees there were in the garden, but I think it's safe to say there were more than one. God says, "You can freely eat from every tree except the tree of the knowledge of good and evil." One command. One tree to avoid. Adam's entire purity came down to one simple command, "Don't eat that fruit!" Whether God gave this command to Adam only and he was left to communicate it to Eve depends on your view of the chronology of Genesis.

All we know is this; they were given the God sized purpose of tending and caring for the garden. They were commanded to enjoy fruit from every tree except *one*. They were naked and felt no shame. They were also told to be fruitful and multiply. Literally, they were commanded by God to have sex!

This is getting better by the second, right? Adam, had it made! Trapped in paradise, surrounded by delicious food, alone with a naked woman who is uninhibited by shame, and a command to have sex. Hello. I should have your attention now.

Here they were, tending the Garden, living in luxury, with everything they need provided for them. Even having each other was a gift from God. They were free to enjoy all that God created, including each other, with just one tree to avoid.

Genesis 3:1-4 [1] **The serpent was the shrewdest of all the wild animals the LORD God had made. One day he asked the woman, "Did God really say you must not eat the fruit from any of the trees in the garden?"** [2] **"Of course we may eat fruit from the trees in the garden," the woman replied.** [3] **"It's only the fruit from the tree in the middle of the garden that we are not allowed to eat. God said, 'You must not eat it or even touch it; if you do, you will die.'"** [4] **"You won't die!" the serpent replied to the woman.**

And the devil has been using the same lie ever since. "You won't die. Sin won't hurt you. Sin doesn't separate you from God. Sin doesn't cause any damage."

Genesis 3:5 [5] **"God knows that your eyes will be opened as soon as you eat it, and you will be like God, knowing both good and evil."**

Which is partially true, right? The devil's not an idiot. He covers up his lies by speaking partial truths. Here he starts with a lie, "You won't die." Then he covers it up with a truth, "Your eyes will be opened, and you'll be like God, knowing both good and evil." Essentially, what the devil is saying to them is the same thing he says to us when it comes to our purity. "God's holding out on you. He's keeping the best for Himself. He's limiting your freedom."

It was true that their eyes would be opened, and it was true that they would know both good and evil, but the being like God part was the furthest thing from the truth. In fact, they were about to find out the truth. Adam and Eve, in their pre-sin state, were closer to being like God than any other human being (excluding Jesus Himself, who was fully God and fully man) would be.

Genesis 3:6a [6] **The woman was convinced. She saw that the tree was beautiful and its fruit looked delicious, and she wanted the wisdom it would give her. So she took some of the fruit and ate it. Then she gave some to her husband, who was with her, and he ate it, too.**

I bet it was delicious. I bet when she bit into that fruit it tasted amazing. Maybe in that moment it was even better than any fruit she had previously eaten. That's why she shared some with Adam. That's how sin works, right?

Sin is fun, exciting, and exhilarating. It's why we're drawn to it. Anyone who tells you that sin isn't fun isn't doing it right. It feels good. It's delicious. It satisfies. It does all those things…for a moment, but then it's gone. The only thing that remains is darkness, emptiness, condemnation and shame.

As I shared earlier in the book, I know first-hand the shame that sin, especially sexual sin brings. I've been in a place of darkness, emptiness, and condemnation that was brought on by my own sinful choices. Whether it's sexual sin or not, all of us have experienced the same thing.

Geneses 3:7 [7] At that moment their eyes were opened, and they suddenly felt shame at their nakedness. So they sewed fig leaves together to cover themselves.

Men pay attention to what I'm about to say. God gave us a command to be pure and we've been chasing pleasure ever since. It's time for us to get our purity back. It's time for us to rise-up, take what God intended and start living it out with intention. Purity won't just happen in our lives, we must be diligent in our pursuit of it.

For the most part, we can be aggressive as men. I believe God gave us that aggression as a good thing. It's our aggression that causes us to defend the weak and fight for the rights of others. It fuels our curiosity, creativity, competitiveness, and sense of adventure. It's our aggression that even moves us to pursue the person we are attracted to. The devil, though, has taken what God started within us, our aggression, and has twisted it for his own gain.

The devil is *not* a creator. He can't create anything. We need to understand this. The devil is powerful, but his power is limited. He's a master at taking what God created as good and twisting it for evil. It is God who created our sexuality. It is God who designed sex to be pleasurable, desirable, and a spiritual bonding agent between a man and woman in marriage.

> PURITY WON'T JUST HAPPEN IN OUR LIVES, WE MUST BE DILIGENT IN OUR PURSUIT OF IT.

The devil didn't create sex, he only twisted our sexuality into a sinful and destructive thing, and destructive it is!

Many great relationships, marriages, careers, bank accounts, and families have been brought down by our twisted sexuality. Prisons are filled with men who used their aggression to satisfy their own sensual lusts. Support groups, recovery programs, and entire educational curriculums have been created in the effort to rescue men from the grips of sexual addictions. It's an epidemic, even among Christian men, and we are being destroyed by it.

THE POWER OF GOD IS POINTLESS UNLESS IT PARTNERS WITH PRACTICES WE PUT IN OUR LIVES.

So how do we break free? How do we get our purity back? I'm not talking about just forgiveness by the way. Forgiveness is available for all our sexual sin, and for some of you, you might need to start there.

No matter how you've lived your sexual life, you can start brand new today. There is no sin God can't forgive and there is no stronghold He can't overcome. You might need to seek God for forgiveness and get a fresh start right now, but that's not only what I'm talking about.

I'm not talking about getting purity into our hearts, I'm talking about living *in* purity *with* our lives! Yes, we need the power of God, but trying to live in purity without God's power will only end in frustration and disappointment. The power of God is pointless unless it partners with practices we put in our lives.

1 Thessalonians 4:7 says **God has called us to live holy lives, not impure lives.**

We all know how to be impure, don't we? No one needs to teach men how to do that. Impurity finds us. It seeks us out. It seems to be lurking around every corner. That's how the enemy works. So again, how do we break free? How do we get our purity back?

If we are going to live holy lives, especially when it comes to our sexuality, we've got to rise-up and use the aggression God gave us toward the purity He expects of us.

Did you know God has already hard wired us as men with everything we need to pursue purity? We just need to acknowledge it, and then access it for its intended purpose.

2 Peter 1:3 By his divine power, God has given us *everything* we need for living a godly (pure) life. We have received all of this by coming to know him, the one who called us to himself by means of his marvelous glory and excellence. (emphasis added)

The Rules Of The Game

In the next chapter, we're going to see the story of someone in the Bible who got it right, by having a game-plan to win the battle of purity. You can't win without a game-plan. Like any game though, you need to know the "rules of the game." It would be nearly impossible to create a game-plan to win a football game if you only knew the rules for baseball. So, before we talk about defeating sexual sin, I think we need to define it.

I believe you can lump all sexual sin into three categories:

1. Pre-Marital sex or sexual activity
2. Extra-marital sex or sexual activity
3. Same-sex sex or sexual activity

The reason I'm using "sexual activity" and not just "sex" to define sexual sin is two-fold.

First, the act of sexual intercourse is not the only sin in our sexuality. I hear people say things like, "Oral sex isn't sex!" Do you realize how stupid that sounds when you use the word "sex" in the description? Or, "Pornography doesn't hurt anybody. It's just an image." (See Appendix 1) Sexual sin goes far beyond, or should I say, starts long before the act of intercourse.

Second, I want to make it abundantly clear that attraction itself is *not* a sin. This is why it's so important to use the words "Same-sex *sex* or sexual *activity*."

Being gay (attracted to the same sex) is not a sin in and of itself, just like me being attracted to another woman is not a sin. We may not get a choice in who we're attracted to, but we do have a choice in what we do with that attraction. That is where our focus needs to be.

I am not an expert on the LGBTQ discussion, and I don't have the time or knowledge to dive into everything here. I have, however, been incredibly helped by some amazing resources out there written for "just such a time as this" (Esther 4:14) in our culture.

If you'd like some insight and help on the LGBTQ discussion, or if you or someone you know is gay, I would highly recommend several resources for you to pursue:

1. *"Single, Gay, Christian: A personal journey of faith and sexual identity"* by Gregory Coles. In this book, Gregory shares his own story of being gay, yet choosing to pursue the purity of God's sexual design in Scripture. I was so inspired in my own purity by the pursuit of it in his life.

2. *"People To Be Loved: Why homosexuality is more than an issue"* by Preston Sprinkle. In my opinion, Preston is the leading voice on understanding what the Bible says about LGBTQ people, and how we should love and treat them in the Church. He has a book for parents and teens called, *"Living In A Gray World."* I had our entire staff read the latter. It was so helpful!

3. The Center For Faith, Sexuality & Gender is also an incredible resource for these discussions. You can access their resources at www.centerforfaith.com.

Now, to make sure you understand the framework I'm coming from, "sexual activity" includes: 1. Any intentional action that can lead to orgasm (including but not limited to intercourse, oral sex, masturbation, "dry humping", etc.) 2. Sexually touching or caressing any body part on someone else that is normally covered in clothing. (Breasts, genitalia, buttocks, etc.) 3. Viewing pornographic or sexually explicit images, videos or movies. 4. Reading or engaging in erotic literature of any kind. 5. Fantasizing sexually or lusting after another person who is not your opposite sex spouse.

Now, this is not about defining all sexuality or explaining the nuances behind it. There are other great books, information, or sermons out there that focus on that, which you could easily find. If you're interested, you can read Appendix 1 to learn a little more about the truth and effects of pre-marital sex, pornography, masturbation and more.

I'm writing this from the assumption that our sexuality and sexual sin has already been defined for us by Scripture. You don't have to agree with this assumption, you just need to understand this is where I'm writing from.

According to Scripture, God designed sex to be enjoyed between one man and one woman, within the bond of marriage for a lifetime. Now, you might argue that the Bible doesn't say "Pre-marital sex is wrong." That's because you're only looking for a negative statement.

You're right, you won't find a "Thou shalt not have pre-marital sex" statement in the Bible, but you will find a God given standard for marriage. God honoring sexual activity is only expressed in Scripture through a marriage between one man and one woman.

In Matthew 19, Jesus makes his clearest statement about marriage and sexuality in his answer to a question the Pharisees were asking. They were grilling Jesus about divorce by asking, is it permissible or is it not? Jesus didn't give a "yes" or "no" answer. His answer actually reveals His definition of marriage and sexuality.

Jesus didn't have to give this definition by the way. He was asked about divorce, not marriage. But in his answer, He gives his standard for marriage, divorce, *and* sex:

Matthew 19:4-6 **[4]** **"Haven't you read the Scriptures?" Jesus replied. "They record that from the beginning 'God made them male and female.'[1]" [5] And he said, "'This explains why a man leaves his father and mother and is joined to his wife, and the two are united into one.' [6] Since they are no longer two but one, let no one split apart what God has joined together."**

The phrase, "united into one," is a sexual phrase as much as it is a spiritual, relational or emotional one. Other versions say, "The two become one flesh." You follow me, right? We don't need flip charts or the local Jr. High health teacher to explain, do we?

Yes, sex is meant for procreation, and yes sex is designed to be pleasurable, but Jesus is taking marriage and sex to a whole new level here. In the act of love making, two people are made one. That's why it's only intended for marriage. Sex is intended for marriage, and in part, marriage is intended for sex.

Here in Matthew 19, Jesus is quoting Genesis 2:24. In Genesis, God institutes marriage by bringing a man and woman together as one. The word "one" used in Genesis is the Hebrew word "Echad" (ekh-awd'). Echad is a deep and mysterious word essentially meaning, "fused together at the deepest level."[2] In sex, when two people come together, they are fused at the deepest level.

With one word, "echad," God defines sex as more than just physical, and marriage as more than just relational. When we have any kind of sexual experience, it affects every part of who we are. It is a bonding of two people into one entity, heart, soul, mind, and body. The word echad is the same word God chooses to use when describing Himself in the book of Deuteronomy.

Deuteronomy 6:4 Hear, O Israel: The Lord our God, the Lord is one (Echad).

So, God's view and God's definition of sex is much greater than cultures view, or even the Churches view of sex. It is not just an activity that we pursue or engage in for pleasure. It's so much more powerful, and so much better than that. As the Father, Son, and Holy Spirit are One, inseparable, so when two people have sex, they are inseparable. Forever linked together, body, soul, and spirit.

Inside of marriage, can you see how this depth of connection is both beautiful and necessary? Why do you think so many couples struggle to have a healthy sex life in marriage? Because our enemy knows how great sex is *for* a marriage. Sex, inside of marriage, takes two people, and won't let them drift from one another. It helps bind them together. It keeps them "one." Sex is a way of expressing our love, inside of marriage, the way God designed for a specific reason.

Outside of marriage though, this can literally tear us apart. Sex was designed by God to be expressed in marriage, therefore outside of marriage it turns people into objects of self-gratification. Every time you engage in and walk away from a sexual partner or experience, you are tearing "echad", leaving a part of you with them and taking a part of them with you.

This is why before we're married the enemy does all he can to bring us together sexually, but after we're married he does all he can to keep us apart. Sex is a weapon! When used properly, it is a weapon for good. When used negatively, it is a weapon for destruction.

I don't mean to conjure up any painful memories here, but this is why people who are molested or raped, even at an early age, are still affected by it decades later. It's more than a physical act that was done to them. The victims of sexual abuse, while completely innocent themselves, can sometimes suffer from emotional, relational, spiritual, and social scars for the rest of their lives. In the most damaging of ways, they are connected to their abuser.

Some of you are starting to make sense of a lot of your life right now. This is why you will never meet a person who says, "Boy, I sure wish I had sex with more people before I got married." Or, "I sure wish I jacked off more." Or, "I sure wish I looked at more porn." It literally tears you to pieces.

With that definition and design of sexuality in mind, every time you read "sexual immorality" or "Fornication" in the New Testament, it is talking about *all* sexual activity outside of God's intended design. That's why I can take verses like the following, and dozens more, and believe they apply to my above definition of "sexual activity":

Hebrews 13:4 - Marriage should be honored by all, and the marriage bed kept pure, for God will judge the adulterer and all the sexually immoral. (NIV)

Marriage should be honored by all! The last time I checked, "all" includes those who aren't married yet, as well as those who are. The marriage bed (all sexual activity), is meant for a married couple only, inside of God's design.

Now, that can sound like a pretty hard rule, especially if you're reading this as a single person. Singleness is one of those topics our modern Church hasn't always handled well, despite the fact that both the Bible and centuries of Church history have held it in high regard. Jesus even speaks of some who "choose not to marry for the sake of the Kingdom of Heaven" (Matthew 19:12), raising singleness, even life-long celibacy, to a position of honor.

IF WE CHOOSE TO LIVE IN PURITY BEFORE WE'RE MARRIED THERE IS A MUCH GREATER CHANCE THAT WE'LL LIVE IN PURITY AFTER WE'RE MARRIED.

As men, the thought of never gratifying our sexual desires, or even waiting until marriage can sound nearly impossible. I'll be the first to say it's hard (pun intended), but I'll also be the first to say that it's worth it. Regardless of why you are single—divorced, widowed, never married, celibate; whether gay or straight—to preserve sex for the God-given boundaries of marriage, while challenging, is the most life-giving choice because it is the only choice that honors God, the giver of life.

So, here is what we need to understand. We keep the marriage bed pure long before we lay in it with our spouse. If we choose to live in purity before we're married there is a much greater chance that we'll live in purity after we're married.

1 Corinthians 7:2-3 **²But because there is so much sexual immorality each man should have his own wife, and each woman should have her own husband. ³The husband should fulfill his wife's sexual needs, and the wife should fulfill her husband's needs.**

1 Corinthians 7:8-9 **⁸ Now to the unmarried and the widows I say: It is good for them to stay unmarried, as I do. ⁹But if they cannot control themselves, they should marry, for it is better to marry than to burn with passion.**

If it wasn't "wrong" for a widow or single person to seek sexual satisfaction outside of their marriage partner, why did God, through Paul, command them to be married first?

1 Corinthians 6:15-17 [15] **Don't you realize that your bodies are actually parts of Christ? Should a man take his body, which is part of Christ, and join it to a prostitute? Never!** [16] **And don't you realize that if a man joins himself to a prostitute, he becomes one body with her? For the Scriptures say, "The two are united into one."**

> YOU SEE, TRUE PLEASURE IS NOT THE OPPOSITE OF PURITY, IT'S THE OUTCOME OF IT.

Matthew 5:27-28 [27] **"You have heard the commandment that says, 'You must not commit adultery.'** [28] **But I say, anyone who even looks at a woman with lust has already committed adultery with her in his heart.**

Those are five Scriptures out of dozens in the New Testament where we are called to a live a life of sexual purity, experiencing the gift of sexual activity within God's design of marriage only. All sexual activity, outside of God's created order, is sinful. It's impure. I know this may sound prude, naïve, old fashioned, and even harsh to some people, but that's the furthest thing from reality.

As followers of Jesus, it's not just that we can't have sex until we're married, it's that we aren't created for that. This is not about God's demands as much as it is about God's design. You see, true pleasure is not the opposite of purity, it's the outcome of it. God never calls us to pursue what is not most pleasurable in our lives.

Like the fruit on the tree in the Garden, God did not put restrictions on our sexuality to limit our pleasure but to unleash its full potential. Will sexual activity outside of marriage or before marriage still feel good? Should I even answer that? *Yes!* Yes, it will feel good, but it cannot fulfill what we are looking for.

Like guardrails on a highway are meant to protect us and keep us safe, so are God's instructions about sex. No one wants us to enjoy our sexuality more than God. He is the architect of it. He knows how it works the best and how it satisfies the most.

I know it sounds strange, but no one is more thrilled with a healthy, thriving, satisfying, pure sex life than God. So how does the enemy deceive us into messing it up? We withhold sex from our spouse inside of God's design (marriage), or we pursue sexual activity outside of His design.

With that in mind, what if we had a game-plan for purity? What would that look like? We better have one. You can be sure that our enemy has a game-plan for our impurity! He is lurking around every corner, like a roaring lion, looking for men to devour (1 Peter 5:8). So, as men, if everything rises and falls on purity, we better be taking this seriously.

The principles I'm going to share in the next chapter will work on all areas of sin, but I want to focus specifically on the area of our sexual sin. It's time for us to rise-up and use our aggression *for* purity and *against* sin in our lives.

This is my declaration!

P.S. I rarely read the Appendix portions of any book, so I hesitate to add them to mine, but in this instance, I believe it may be helpful. For many people, while you might be failing in one of the areas of sexual sin we've talked about, you're at least on the same page with what sexual sin is and why it should be avoided. For others though, you aren't on the same page. While you might see the Scriptural basis for my position, you still don't understand what all the fuss is about.

Well, not only is there a Scriptural basis for sexual purity, but there is a scientific one as well. I didn't want to weigh the chapters down with statistics and information so in Appendix 1, I offer information garnered from extensive research about pornography, masturbation, pre-marital sex, and co-habitation. In that appendix, I also offer further personal thoughts and experiences about the issue of purity.

FIVE

A GAME-PLAN FOR PURITY

Until we understand how our impurity offends God, we will never feel obligated to run from it ourselves and run we must.

As a man, I am convinced that you either have before, are now, or will in the future struggle with sexual purity. We might struggle in different ways but we all struggle. As stated before, we are sexual beings. There is no doubt about that. It's the way we're wired. One survey found that five out of ten men think about sex "very often" throughout the day. The other five had to have the question repeated because they were thinking about sex. (I made that up but come on now, that's funny!)

Sex is awesome! We've established that. If you are married, you have God's permission and blessing to enjoy what He has created with your wife. The devil though, has taken what was meant to be a wonderful gift in marriage and has twisted it into a weapon of mass destruction.

Like he did in the garden, he has twisted the truth of our sexuality. He has tricked, deceived, and manipulated us into using our aggression to please ourselves instead of protecting our purity. Instead of our sexuality enhancing relationships he has led us down a path where it has annihilated them.

It's time to change directions. It's time to rise-up, implement a game-plan, and partner with the power of the Holy Spirit to gain victory in this area of our lives. It's time to use our aggression as an attack on sin instead of an acceptance of it.

Joseph had a game-plan. Joseph models for us a game-plan for purity, and he was very aggressive with it. Of all the lessons we see in Josephs life; forgiveness, faithfulness, trust, vision, promise, Sovereignty of God, and more, his example of purity has been the most helpful for me. Here in Genesis 39, a game-plan for purity unfolds before our very eyes.

Genesis 39:6-12 [6] **So Potiphar gave Joseph complete administrative responsibility over everything he owned. With Joseph there, he didn't worry about a thing—except what kind of food to eat! Joseph was a very handsome and well-built young man,** (About 90% men reading this just said about themselves, "Oh, he must have looked a lot like me.") [7] **and Potiphar's wife soon began to look at him lustfully. "Come and sleep with me," she demanded.** [8] **But Joseph refused. "Look,"** **he told her, "my master trusts me with everything in his entire household.** [9] **No one here has more authority than I do. He has held back nothing from me except you, because you are his wife. How could I do such a wicked thing? It would be a great sin against God."** [10] **She kept putting pressure on Joseph day after day, but he refused to sleep with her, and he kept out of her way as much as possible.** [11] **One day, however, no one else was around when he went in to do his work.** [12] **She came and grabbed him by his cloak, demanding, "Come on, sleep with me!" Joseph tore himself away, but he left his cloak in her hand as he ran from the house.**

Some men are reading this thinking something had to be different about Joseph, or something had to be incredibly wrong with Potiphar's wife to turn down a proposal like this. Potiphar was a man of position and power in Egypt, which meant his wife would have been highly sought after. Men of position and power could have any woman they chose, so his wife would have been the desire of many throughout the land, including guys like Joseph.

Here she was, a woman of desire, throwing herself at him. Who would have known if he gave in? She had gotten away with her advances already, surely, she could hide the adultery as well. She wouldn't make such an audacious proposal without first formulating a plan to protect the secret. She had to be completely stunned by Joseph's response. Not only did he refuse to sleep with her, he ran from the situation.

What made Joseph run? Or a better question, why did Joseph run and how did he have the strength to do so? Joseph wasn't some random anomaly in manhood that was immune to temptation. This wasn't a sexual attraction issue, this was a spiritual attitude issue!

Joseph was a man like you and me. As a man, he had urges and desires for sex like any other human being. God had not taken away those desires or removed the ability to act on them, Joseph simply made a different choice.

> UNTIL WE UNDERSTAND HOW OUR IMPURITY OFFENDS GOD, WE WILL NEVER FEEL OBLIGATED TO RUN FROM IT OURSELVES AND RUN WE MUST.

The key to Joseph's game-plan, and ultimately the key to ours, is found in the statement he made to Potiphar's wife after her initial proposition: **"It would be a great sin against God."** (Genesis 39:9) You see, Joseph recognized what he was after most, and we must as well.

In one statement, "It would be a great sin against God," Joseph revealed that his ultimate desire was to please God. In fact, Joseph's desire for pleasing God was greater than his desire to please himself, therefore he ran!

Here is a truth for us: Until we understand how our impurity offends God, we will never feel obligated to run from it ourselves and run we must.

As men, we are fighters. That's part of our aggression. We even use the "fight" language when it comes to sin. It's found in the Bible as well. We are told to "fight the good fight" of the faith (1 Timothy 6:12). Paul uses a boxing analogy when talking about the battle against sin (1 Corinthians 9:24-27). However, when it comes to sexual sin we are given a different kind of game-plan.

1 Corinthians 6:18-20 [18] **Run from sexual sin! No other sin so clearly affects the body as this one does. For sexual immorality is a sin against your own body.** [19] **Don't you realize that your body is the temple of the Holy Spirit, who lives in you and was given to you by God? You do not belong to yourself,** [20] **for God bought you with a high price. So you must honor God with your body.**

Run from sexual sin! Don't fight it, don't flirt with it, don't fool around with it, but run from it.

Joseph understood this principle long before it was penned by the Apostle Paul. This Scripture was written on his heart before it was ever read on paper. Joseph recognized what he was after. He was after The Lord! His desire to please God was greater than his desire to please himself, and it caused him to run. He *chose* to run.

Sexual sin is always a choice. It never "just happens". No matter how much you want to say, "It just happened," we all know that's not the case. It's not like you found yourself in a room with someone and then, "Woah, how did that happen? We were both in the room and somehow we just had sex."

At some point in all sexual sin a choice is made to pursue self over the Savior. I can't pursue sexual sin and pursue Jesus at the same time. To pursue Jesus, I must turn from sexual sin, and to pursue sexual sin I must turn from Jesus.

I'm either pursuing sin or the Savior. I'm either seeking to please God or I'm seeking to please myself. Which, by the way, pleasing God is what will ultimately bring the greatest pleasure to ourselves. God's not against pleasure, He's against impurity.

Let me pause for a moment and address the women. Somewhere, there is a single woman reading this and your "man" has been drawing you down the path of sexual sin. The devil has convinced you that, "He loves you!" and that love is what's caused you to give in. But let me challenge you with something different.

If he truly loved you, he would be leading you toward Jesus and not away from Him. Every time he leads you toward sexual sin he is pulling you away from Jesus, which means if he was leading you toward Jesus he would be pulling you away from sexual sin.

Listen ladies, if he is ok pursuing sexual immorality with you before you're married, what makes you think he won't pursue sexual immorality against you after you're married? (The same thing could be true for single guys who have a girlfriend pulling you toward sin, but in most instances that is not the case. If it is, my thoughts for you are the same.)

"How could I do such a wicked thing? It would be a great sin against God." (Genesis 39:9)

Is pursuing Jesus the first-priority in my purity? How do I even know? Ultimately, we must run from sexual sin, but our running starts long before the opportunity to sin arises. Joseph recognized what he was after, He was after the Lord, but he also refused to even get close to sin. Genesis 39:10 says:

Genesis 39:10 [10] She (Potiphar's wife) **kept putting pressure on Joseph day after day, but he refused to sleep with her, and he kept out of her way as much as possible.**

First off, I guarantee that when you try and break away from sexual sin it's not going to be easy. You can't just decide to be done with sexual sin, and it's done. You can't say a prayer and expect it to be over. The enemy doesn't give up just because we go the other way.

Like Potiphar's wife, when we refuse to satisfy our sinful desires the enemy will seek out more opportunities to trip us up. The moment you decide to pursue Christ first, the pressure, temptations, and even opportunities to sin will increase. It might be painful, it's going to be messy, and I promise it will be hard work, but you can do it.

More than the pressure to give in though, I want you to notice the purpose in which Joseph used his aggression to attack impurity.

"...and he kept out of her way as much as possible." (Genesis 39:10)

This one practice alone could set so many men free. When opportunities for sexual sin already seek us out, why in the world would we set ourselves up for more opportunities by getting closer to it? We've got to refuse to even get close to sexual sin.

When I was a youth pastor, the number one question I got from young people about sex was, "How far is too far?" I don't remember who I first heard this answer from, but I've been using it ever since: "That question is too far!"

When we ask the question, "How far is too far?" what we are really asking is, "How close to sin can I actually get without sinning? How close to the line can I be before I cross over?" It's what I call Crocodile Hunter theology.

Remember the Crocodile Hunter? His name was Steve Irwin, and he became famous as an animal conservationist and fearless risk taker in the animal kingdom.[1] Unfortunately, his love for animals led to his untimely death, but his risk taking is what I remember most.

My wife and I used to watch his weekly television program and I would repeatedly comment on how crazy this guy was. One time, I remember watching him lie on the ground with his face by a hole. Then, in that classic Australian accent, he said something like, "In this hole is the deadliest snake in the world. We're miles from the closest hospital or medical services so one bite from this bloke and I'll die."

I yelled at the TV, "Then why are you by the hole?" Every episode, Steve would put himself directly in a situation where, "I could die," and men, we're doing the same thing every day!

With that extra click on the computer, glance at the gym, comment to the attractive co-worker, stop on the channel, or secret conversation through text or email. With every advance from 1st base to 2nd. With every excuse; "It's too late to go home, just stay the night here. We're different, we can stop before it's too far. We're not actually having sex."

Whatever it is. With every excuse we make, inching closer and closer to the line, we are subconsciously saying, "If this bites me, I'll die." And as men, we wonder why we're dead inside.

Both Adam and Eve made this fatal mistake, and it led to their deaths. Apparently, they were standing right by the tree when the serpent tempted them, for it says, **"⁶The woman was convinced. She saw that the tree was beautiful and its fruit looked delicious, and she wanted the wisdom it would give her. So she took some of the fruit and ate it. Then she gave some to her husband, who was with her, and he ate it, too."** (Genesis 3:6)

Are we really surprised they ate the fruit? What conversations led up to this moment? What were they saying and thinking as they stood there? "How close to the tree can we get before we actually break God's command? I'm just looking at the fruit. What do you think it tastes like? God never said we couldn't stand next to it. I wonder if I can smell it?" It's exactly what Solomon says in Proverbs 6:27-29:

Proverbs 6:27-29 ²⁷ Can a man scoop a flame into his lap and not have his clothes catch on fire? ²⁸ Can he walk on hot coals and not blister his feet? ²⁹ So it is with the man who sleeps with another man's wife. He who embraces her will not go unpunished.

When we flirt with the spark of sin, especially sexual sin, we are eventually going to find ourselves getting burned. The Apostle Paul even refers to sexual desire as, "burning with lust." (1 Corinthians 7:9)

WHEN WE FLIRT WITH THE SPARK OF SIN, ESPECIALLY SEXUAL SIN, WE ARE EVENTUALLY GOING TO FIND OURSELVES GETTING BURNED.

If Joseph wasn't tempted to say "yes," then why did he keep out of her way as much as possible? Have you ever thought about that? If there was no desire to give in he could have just gone along with his normal, every-day life, but he knew this wasn't business as usual.

Think about it. Joseph was a servant in the house of Potiphar. His job was *in* the house, and Potiphar's wife did not have a job outside the house. So, every day, his own job brought him to a place of temptation. Joseph probably had a routine in the home. Most likely he knew how to get from point A to point B the fastest, and where he needed to be at every moment of the day.

Now, to avoid the temptress, he had to go out of his way to find new routes in the home. He had to rearrange his duties, reorganize his day, and reset some routines. No doubt it was uncomfortable, inconvenient, and annoying, but if he was going to remain pure he needed to refuse to even get close. He had to get aggressive with his game-plan.

Men, instead of asking, "How far is too far?" when it comes to sexual sin. Instead of saying, "How close to the line can I get?" What if we asked, "How close to Jesus can I be today?" I promise you, in your sexual life, Jesus is nowhere close to that line.

When you recognize what you're after - Jesus - you will begin to refuse to even get close. It doesn't mean the opportunities to sin will cease, it just means that your response to them will begin to change. This leads to the last thing Joseph had in his game-plan.

Genesis 39:12b Joseph tore himself away, but he left his cloak in her hand as he ran from the house.

Notice, the dude didn't just run away, he ran away leaving his cloak (outer garment) in her hand. At best, he was running away in his underwear.

He recognized what he was after, he was after the Lord. He refused to even get close, setting extreme boundaries in his life. He resolved to do whatever it takes. Joseph was willing to look like a fool in the land in order to remain faithful to the Lord.

What are you willing to do in order to remain faithful? I don't know how far it was for Joseph to get from this place of temptation to a tunic, but someone had to see him half naked. Someone had to see him darting out of that room running to safety. How foolish did that look? How foolish will it look for us to run from the room as well?

If we are going to break free from sexual sin, especially if you already find yourself caught in its grasp, we will have to resolve to do whatever it takes. Drastic times call for drastic measures, and some people won't understand.

"You're not going to be alone together? Why would you do that?" "You're getting rid of your computer at home? Isn't that a bit extreme?" "You're putting what kind of software on your devices? Accountability software? Why would you want someone knowing what you're looking at online?" In Matthew 5, Jesus says:

> **JOSEPH WAS WILLING TO LOOK LIKE A FOOL IN THE LAND IN ORDER TO REMAIN FAITHFUL TO THE LORD.**

Matthew 5:27-30 **27 "You have heard the commandment that says, 'You must not commit adultery.' 28 But I say, anyone who even looks at a woman with lust has already committed adultery with her in his heart. 29 So if your eye—even your good eye — causes you to lust, gouge it out and throw it away. It is better for you to lose one part of your body than for your whole body to be thrown into hell. 30 And if your hand—even your stronger hand—causes you to sin, cut it off and throw it away.**

It is better for you to lose one part of your body than for your whole body to be thrown into hell.
This doesn't mean we need a bunch of one-handed cyclops' walking around, it just means we are to take drastic and aggressive measures in our purity. Jesus was telling us that we should do whatever it takes to remain pure. Nothing is too extreme or aggressive when it comes to pursuing purity. Nothing!

The boundaries you need may not be the same as someone else's, but we all need boundaries. Each of us knows our own weaknesses, and our weaknesses determine the measures we should take.

By the way, this isn't about legalism, it's about love. My love for God, my wife, my kids, and my calling, compel me to put boundaries in place that keep me focused on purity. These boundaries don't guarantee my purity, but they certainly keep me pointed towards that goal.

I've personally put a game-plan in place for when I am tempted, and yes, I am still tempted. Some days I don't have to use the game-plan at all, but others, it feels like I'm using it around every corner. (See Appendix 2 and 3 for more about the boundaries I've put in place and what my game-plan for purity looks like. It might help you develop yours.)

Men, it's time to change directions. It's time to rise-up and use the aggression God gave us toward the purity He expects from us. So, I will rise-up and realize what I'm after most, I'm after the Lord! I will refuse to even get close, running from all sexual sin. I will resolve to do whatever it takes, setting extreme boundaries in my life.

This is my declaration!

SIX

TAKING RESPONSIBILITY IN MY LIFE

It's only when we're completely honest about who we are that God's power is completely unleashed into what we do.

Everyone knows that the one thing you don't mess with in a guy's home is the remote control, right? As men, we do lust for power, and there is no greater power when it comes to watching TV than the man's remote.

I'm a flipper. I don't know if you're a flipper, but I'm a flipper. This has nothing to do with gymnastic ability or a vulgar hand gesture, I'm talking about flipping channels. The advent of the DVR has changed this dramatically in my life, but if I'm watching a live program, at each commercial break I start flipping channels to see what else can keep my attention before I go back to the original program. I'm pretty sure I got this from my dad.

My dad is a flipper too. The remote control was a prized possession in our home. I remember the very first remote control we had when I was a kid. It wasn't even wireless. It was connected by a wire to our VCR. (If you don't know what a VCR is Google it or look it up on YouTube)

Before the wired remote, you may have grown up like this as well; us kids were the remote control. Yes, we used to change the channel manually on the TV itself, and the kids were the dad's remote control. (You can YouTube that too. The TV had a knob on the front that you would turn to change the channel.)

I'll never forget the time I messed with my dad's remote. I don't remember what the event was, but I remember it being an important day for the remote control. Maybe it was New Year's Day football or the Super Bowl, I don't remember, but people were at our home, food was prepared, and we were all gathering around the TV to enjoy the program.

I was one of the first to get my plate filled with food, poured a giant cup of pop to enjoy, walked to the recliner in the living room, and began to get situated in my place. I set my cup of pop on the floor to my right, and I set the remote control on the armrest, directly above said cup. As I rocked the recliner back to kick up the footrest, my elbow hit the remote control causing it to flip (pun intended), fall toward the ground, and land in a perfect vertical position in my cup. It was fully submerged.

A wave of panic came over me as I knew how important that remote was to the day. No one was in the room but me, so no one had seen what happened. In seconds, I formulated a plan. I removed the remote control from the pop and was able to get it out of the room un-noticed. I dried it off with a hand towel, made sure it was all cleaned up and ready to go, got back to the living room, placed the remote where it had been, sat in another seat and went on with my day.

Sure enough, a few minutes later my dad entered the room. He promptly took his seat in the recliner, grabbed the remote, didn't notice any residue from the pop, pointed it at the TV and...nothing. As any guy does, he hit the remote, pointed it at the TV, but again, nothing.

Well, now he was on a mission. Removing and re-entering the batteries didn't work. Standing closer to the TV didn't work. Getting new batteries didn't work. I wanted to say, "I'll be the remote dad." But I didn't want to bring any undue attention to myself. I had broken the remote and tried to cover it up. This went on for several minutes, but in spite of my dad's best efforts, the pop had destroyed the remote.

It was then that my dad started asking people, "Do you know what happened to the remote?" He made his rounds, person after person. Everyone was clueless as to what happened to the remote. And then he came to me. "Jeff, do you know what happened to the remote?"

I didn't want to admit my guilt, so I answered his question with a question of my own. Maybe this would get him off my scent. "Um," I said sheepishly, "will pop hurt it?" The look on my dad's face was priceless. He asked, "Will pop hurt it? Why would you ask if pop will hurt it?"

There was no getting out of this one. I knew I was busted. I quickly confessed to what I had done and the cover up that ensued. If I would have just taken responsibility in the first place, this whole ordeal could have been handled in a much easier fashion.

> BIBLICAL MANHOOD PROMOTES GOD AT ANY COST, FOR THE SAKE OF THE WOMEN, CHILDREN, AND ANY PERSON WE'VE BEEN PLACED OVER OR BESIDE.

Men, once we rise-up to finish what was started, find purpose in our pain, get bold in our faith, and become aggressive at purity, we also have to rise-up and take responsibility. Responsibility for the positions of authority we've been given. As men, God has placed us in positions of authority. Please understand, this is not a male chauvinist statement in any way.

Male chauvinism promotes the man at any cost, even at the expense of women, children, and the people they are placed over or beside. Biblical manhood promotes God at any cost, for the sake of the women, children, and any person we've been placed over or beside.

We are called to own up to our failures, be honest about what we've done, respect and honor the authority that's been placed over us, and lead with integrity in the authority that's been given to us.

The role of a man is not to be taken lightly. In fact, I believe there is no greater honor and no higher calling for a man than to live in

Biblical manhood. God has set the highest standards for us, and real men are needed to take the reins, lead the way, forge ahead, make a difference, and it all comes down to this one question: Are we ready to take responsibility?

A real man won't use his authority to advance and promote himself; he takes responsibility for his authority, dies to himself, and lives to advance the cause of Christ for the sake of those around him. So, what do I do to take responsibility? If taking responsibility is the next step, how do I do that?

In Genesis chapter 3, we see in Adam some great truths about responsibility. Adam didn't do a very good job. In fact, he did just about everything wrong. But even in the pitfalls of Adam we are pointed to some profound principles about taking responsibility.

Since the fall of Adam, every man has struggled with abdicating our responsibility to manage the authority that's been given to us, and it is reflected today in our homes, jobs, Churches, and cities all around our country. In an article put out by CNN in 2011 called *"Why men are in trouble"*, it said:

"For the first time in history, women are better educated, more ambitious and arguably more successful than men."[1]

Women now surpass men in college degrees almost 3 to 2 and Women's earnings grew 44% in real dollars from 1970 to 2007, compared with 6% growth for men.

Now listen, I'm all for women getting degrees, earning great jobs, receiving equal pay, and having better positions in the workforce. As a father of three daughters, I pray every day that they would be able to reach any height God has for them, and may nothing stand in their way, especially their gender or some power-hungry man. If you hear this as a slam against women, you're hearing me wrong. I'm using this article, from a secular, liberal source, which sees these realities as signs of a greater problem we have with men, because it goes on to say this:

Men are more distant from family or their children than they have ever been. The out-of-wedlock birthrate is more than 40% in America. In 1960, only 11% of children in the U.S. lived apart from their fathers. In 2010, that share had risen to 27%. Men are also less religious than ever before. According to Gallup polling, 39% of men reported attending Church regularly in 2010, compared to 47% of women.

This decline in founding virtues -- work, marriage, and religion -- has caught the eye of social commentators from all corners. In her seminal article, "The End of Men," Hanna Rosin unearthed the unprecedented role reversal that is taking place today. "Man has been the dominant sex since, well, the dawn of mankind. But for the first time in human history, that is changing—and with shocking speed," writes Rosin.

Man's response has been pathetic. Today, 18-to- 34-year-old men spend more time playing video games a day than 12-to- 17-year-old boys. While women are graduating college and finding good jobs, too many men are not going to work, not getting married and not raising families. Women are beginning to take the place of men in many ways. This has led some to ask: do we even need men?

"Do we even need men?" Not only do we need men, but being real men is an absolute necessity to the future of our society. Not just men by the biological definition, but men by the Biblical definition. Not men in quantity, but men in character.

In order to make that shift, it starts with men in the Church, followers of Jesus, rising-up to take responsibility for the authority we've been given; the authority that God gave to us. So, how do we do that?

First of all, each of us needs to acknowledge where we are. Until we acknowledge where we are we won't be able to move forward to where we need to be, and we definitely won't be able to help other people become who they are called to be.

Remember in Genesis 3, Adam ate the fruit. When he did, his eyes were opened, he felt the shame of his nakedness, sewed fig lives together to cover he and his wife, and then look at what happens next.

Genesis 3:8-9 [8] **When the cool evening breezes were blowing, the man and his wife heard the LORD God walking about in the garden. So they hid from the LORD God among the trees.** [9] **Then the LORD God called to the man, "Where are you?"**

"Where are you?", God asks. That same question which God asked the very first man, I believe He is asking all men today. "Where are you?" That question is a double-entendre. Not only is God asking us personally, "Where are you and why are you hiding," but He's also calling out to men in general, and calling to the manhood inside of us, "Where are you men? Where are you?"

By the way, God didn't need to ask that question, Adam needed to answer it. God already knew where Adam was. God already knows where we are as well. It's not like Adam was so good at hide and seek that he actually found a spot that even God couldn't find. God asked Adam where he was because Adam needed to answer that question, and quite frankly, so do we.

UNTIL I ADMIT WHERE I AM I CAN NEVER MOVE FORWARD TO WHERE GOD WANTS ME TO BE.

Where am I? What am I hiding from? What responsibility has God given me that I need to rise-up and take hold of in my life? Who in my life has God placed me over or beside that I need to take responsibility for their spiritual, emotional, relational or physical well-being? God asked Adam, "Where are you?" and He's asking me the same question today.

Until I admit where I am I can never move forward to where God wants me to be. This leads right into the next thing we need to do to take responsibility, we need to admit who we are.

It might sound like this is the same as the first step, and it's definitely similar, but there is an important separation of the two. One of the reasons we don't want to acknowledge *where* we are is because when we do, we have to also admit *who* we are.

Genesis 3:10 [10] **He** (Adam) **replied, "I heard you walking in the garden, so I hid. I was afraid because I was naked."**

No pun intended here, but that verse is so revealing about who we are as men. One thing we don't ever want to admit is that we are afraid. Yet it is the fear of who we know we are that actually keeps us from acknowledging where we are.

I noticed something for the first time in reading this text. God said, "Where are you?", and Adam replied, "I hid because I was afraid of my nakedness." Adam admitted where he was; he was hiding. He admitted how he was; he was naked. The only thing he didn't admit was who he was, and there is a massive difference.

When God said, "Where are you?" he should have said, "I heard you and I hid because I ate the fruit. I didn't do what You asked. I disobeyed. I sinned against you which makes me a *sinner.*"

I believe too many men are standing naked before all mighty God willing to admit how they are, yet not willing to admit who they are. Still trying to prove, "I can do this on my own. I can fix it. I'll sew fig leaves together, jump behind a tree and no one will notice." We need to respond more like Isaiah and Peter did when they encountered the presence of Almighty God.

> I BELIEVE TOO MANY MEN ARE STANDING NAKED BEFORE ALL MIGHTY GOD WILLING TO ADMIT HOW THEY ARE, YET NOT WILLING TO ADMIT WHO THEY ARE.

Isaiah 1:5 "It's all over! I am doomed, for I am a sinful man. I have filthy lips, and I live among a people with filthy lips. Yet I have seen the King, the Lord of Heaven's Armies."

Luke 5:8 "Oh, Lord, please leave me—I'm such a sinful man."

We should respond more like David did when he finally took responsibility for his affair with Bathsheba.

IT'S ONLY WHEN WE'RE COMPLETELY HONEST ABOUT WHO WE ARE THAT GOD'S POWER IS COMPLETELY UNLEASHED INTO WHAT WE DO.

2 Samuel 12:13 "I have sinned against the Lord."

Psalm 51:4, 7-11 Against you, and you alone, have I sinned; I have done what is evil in your sight. Purify me from my sins, and I will be clean; wash me, and I will be whiter than snow. ⁸Oh, give me back my joy again; you have broken me— now let me rejoice. ⁹Don't keep looking at my sins. Remove the stain of my guilt. ¹⁰Create in me a clean heart, O God. Renew a loyal spirit within me. ¹¹Do not banish me from your presence, and don't take your Holy Spirit from me.

David prayed for restoration, which is exactly what God wants to do for us. God wasn't looking for Adam so He could ridicule him for his sin, He was looking for Adam so He could restore him from his sin. God knows, until I admit who I currently am, He cannot get me to be all that He's called me to be.

Guys, sometimes our greatest act of strength is to admit, "I can't do this on my own God! I can't fix this without You. I can't be who You want me to be or live how You want me to live without Your help. I'm stepping out from behind the tree, and I'm naked. I don't know what to do next. I know I have sinned, I need a Savior and I'm ready to take responsibility in my life. This is where I am, and this is who I am. I am Yours."

This isn't a one-time thing we do in our lives either. This is an everyday thing. Each day, if I'm going to take responsibility in my life, I need to admit where I am and who I am to God. It's only when we're completely honest about who we are that God's power is completely unleashed into what we do.

It may not even be a sin issue that you need to be honest with God about. I don't know where you are, and I don't know who you truly are, only you and God know that. All I know is this, He's asking today, "Where are you?", and He's waiting for a response. We won't ever be able to move forward until we answer that question in our lives.

The last step after admitting where and who we are is to accept all the blame in our life. I'm not talking about accepting the blame for things that were done to us, but like David did, accepting the blame for what I've done against God.

Most often, the place we find ourselves in our life has been determined by the practices of our life. For most of us, if we don't like where we are, we only need to look in the mirror for who to blame.

After Adam admitted he was naked, God asked, **"Who told you that you were naked? Have you eaten from the tree whose fruit I commanded you not to eat?"** (Genesis 3:11)

If I were Adam, I might have tried to change the subject or something. This would be my, "Will pop hurt it?", moment. "Actually God, I didn't notice we were naked until I saw Eve, and holy cow! I mean, the rest of creation is amazing, but You out did Yourself with that one. I see now why You call her 'woman', because *woah man*!" Adam didn't change the subject though, he just tried to shift the blame.

Genesis 3:12-13 **¹²The man replied, "It was the woman you gave me who gave me the fruit, and I ate it." ¹³ Then the LORD God asked the woman, "What have you done?" "The serpent deceived me," she replied. "That's why I ate it."**

Honestly, we've been blaming women ever since, haven't we? Adam could have admitted where he was and even who he was, but he still wasn't willing to accept the blame for what he did. Not only did he blame the woman, but he even blamed God. **"It was the woman that you game me.**" (Genesis 3:12) In other words, "Everything was fine God, until she came along."

Do you realize that even though Eve is the one who first ate the fruit, it appears that the blame rested on Adam? In Genesis 2:15-17, God gave Adam the command to not eat the fruit. We don't know if Eve was present for the command or if Adam was supposed to pass it on to her, all we know was the command was given to Adam and he was placed in authority, with Eve, over the Garden.

Then in chapter 3 of Genesis, we see what are perhaps the saddest and most challenging verses in all of the Bible.

Genesis 3:6-7 ⁶ The woman was convinced. She saw that the tree was beautiful and its fruit looked delicious, and she wanted the wisdom it would give her. So she took some of the fruit and ate it. Then she gave some to her husband, who was *with* her, and he ate it, too. ⁷ At *that* moment their eyes were opened, and they suddenly felt shame at their nakedness. So they sewed fig leaves together to cover themselves. (emphasis added)

Adam was there. He was standing with her when she ate the fruit. All he had to do was take responsibility for the authority he'd been given to lead his wife towards holiness, but he stood there, took the fruit from her, and ate it. I want you to notice, it was when Adam ate the fruit that their eyes were opened. The responsibility was his, and he blew it.

It wasn't the woman's fault that Adam sinned, and it definitely wasn't God's. We really can't even blame the devil. "The devil made me do it," is never a justifiable response. The devil was only doing what he does best, which is deceive. Adam needed to accept all the blame, but he didn't, and we struggle doing the same.

Many times, our wives don't respect us because we've done nothing to earn their respect. Our kids don't follow us because we haven't shown them any reason to trust where they would be led. Leaders don't believe in us because we've done nothing to show them we have the ability to do what they want us to do. We want all the authority without taking any responsibility or accepting any blame.

Let me speak also to the wives for just a moment. I understand, I really do, how frustrating we can be as men. We don't do what you think we should do, focus on what you'd like us to focus on, or live how you believe we should live. Many times, it's because we haven't taken responsibility that causes you to take the lead in the home. I get that. But I want you to notice something in this Scripture.

> WE WANT ALL THE AUTHORITY WITHOUT TAKING ANY RESPONSIBILITY OR ACCEPTING ANY BLAME.

Eve could do nothing to change Adam's life. Nothing! Adam changed because he had an all-knowing God who sought him out, saved him, and set him free. I'm not saying this to all of you, but some of you need to stop asking your husband to change and start asking God to change you!

Don't pray for your husband to change into what you want him to be. Pray for your husband to surrender fully to who Jesus wants Him to be, and then commit yourself to submit to God through the process. In doing this your husband won't become who you dream he can be, but who God dreams he can be, which is actually all you'll ever need him to be in the first place.

I don't know who to credit this to, but I've heard it many times before. Inside of every man is a king or a kid. Wives, the one that you speak to the loudest is the one who will come alive. If you want a good king in your man, start speaking to the king inside him.

Deep down, I believe every man is dying to take responsibility, but the longer we wait to do it, the more a part of us dies. So, what do you say men? Is there an area in your life that you need to take responsibility for? Do you need to acknowledge where you are, admit who you are, or accept any blame?

Jesus was the ultimate example of this. He wasn't some weak spirited, jelly fish backboned kind of guy. He stood strong in the face of oppression. He stared his enemies in the face. He lived and led for everything that was true and right. He protected the unprotected, served the un-servable, and loved the unlovable. He didn't use His authority to advance Himself, instead, He died to Himself, took up His cross and sacrificed for the sake of everyone else.

I don't say all this to make us feel like losers, I say this in the hopes that it will awaken the leader within us.

Because I've been given authority in my life, I will choose to rise-up and take responsibility for that authority, igniting a fire in my heart to be all that God sees I can be. I will acknowledge where I am, admit who I am, and accept all the blame from what I've done. I will use my authority to promote God at any cost, for the sake of anyone He places me over or beside.

This is my declaration!

SEVEN

TAKING RESPONSIBILITY IN MY HOME

The responsibility to lead our homes well is second only to our responsibility to lead ourselves well.

In December of 1994, I attended a youth conference in Colorado Springs, along with our home Church from Oklahoma. My good friend and future brother in law, Ryan, was on the trip with us. Ryan, being in Jr. High at the time, naturally looked up to me as a Sophomore in college who was also dating his sister.

After the conference was over, our youth pastor had scheduled a one-day ski trip to a nearby resort. This was Ryan's first-time skiing, and being the caring, concerned, older friend I was, I thought, "I'll take him under my wing and use this opportunity to teach a young man how to ski. I'll 'take responsibility' for this." That would have been all well and good if I knew how to ski myself.

At that point in my life, I had been skiing a grand total of…drum roll…one time. That one time was eight years prior, and it was at a little tiny ski area outside of Buffalo, WY, where the skiing isn't quite comparable to the giant ski resorts Colorado has to offer.

Ryan was a bit nervous and unsure of himself, which is to be expected for any first-time skier. So, I did the typical man thing by opening my mouth and promising to do something I was incapable of doing. "I'll teach you how to ski," I said. Famous last words.

So, we rented all the gear, bypassed paying for the real lesson, and headed for the slopes. As we got in line, I continued boasting about myself while also trying to build him up in his skiing courage. We approached the front of the line where a little girl, maybe 9 or 10 years old, asked if she could join us on this three-person lift. We obliged and started our ride up the hill.

On the lift, it was me in the middle, Ryan to my left, and this little innocent girl on the right-hand side of me. The whole way up the lift I'm telling Ryan, "Now you just put your skis down, bend your knees, and go." Again, "Put your skis down, bend your knees, and go." That was my grand skiing instructions, "Put your ski's down, bend your knees, and go."

I actually had no idea what I was talking about, but at least I sounded like I did because Ryan was paying full attention. I also noticed that the girl next to me was looking up to me. I was feeling pretty good about myself at this point.

Ryan was hanging on my every word; this girl was looking up to me, this was going to be a shining moment in my life. Looking back, I now realize she was looking up, not because I was someone to be looked up to, but because I was taller than her.

We get towards the top of the lift and I ask Ryan, "Are you ok? Remember, just put your skis down, bend your knees, and go." We arrived at the top, put our ski's down, bent our knees, and as I'm ready to bask in the glory of my ski instructing ability, *boom*, both my ski's go flying out from underneath me at the same time. It was like I put my ski's down on an ice-skating rink.

Time suspended for a moment. Like a slow-motion scene in a movie, my body went parallel to the ground, every extremity began to flail, and not only did my out of control body take myself out, but I took the poor little girl beside me out as well.

I actually landed on top her, my skis were tangled up, snow was in my face and I couldn't get off the ground. I caused so much chaos that they had to stop the lift behind me to help me up. All the while, Ryan just put his skis down, bent his legs, and went. By the time I could look up to see if he was ok, he caught my eye with a look of,

"Seriously dude?" Needless to say, he didn't ask for my help the rest of the day.

Men, that to me is the picture of our homes if we don't get this right. In our homes, God has entrusted us with people to lead, love, and protect. For those of us who are married, this would be our wives. For those with kids, they are included too.

When we refuse to rise-up and take responsibility in our lives. When we refuse to acknowledge where we are, admit who we are, or accept the blame for what we've done, we are only leading ourselves and our families into chaos. The responsibility to lead our homes well is second only to our responsibility to lead ourselves well.

Fortunately, in the case of my story, it was only skiing. Unfortunately, in our lives our faith and our families, too many times, we are just like I was on that slope. Oh, we can talk a big game, but when it comes to actually leading well, we either take someone down with us, or the person we are supposed to lead stands there in disgust saying, "Really? I'll just handle it myself."

Guys, we have been given authority in our homes, but until we take responsibility to use that authority to honor God and build up the people He has entrusted us with, we will never be able to lead them to be all that God sees they can be.

> THE RESPONSIBILITY TO LEAD OUR HOMES WELL IS SECOND ONLY TO OUR RESPONSIBILITY TO LEAD OURSELVES WELL.

For men, Ephesians chapter 5 and the first part of chapter 6 might be some of the most important texts in all the Bible. In this one section, Paul challenges us to live in the light while we are under the authority of Jesus and His Word. He challenges us to live by the power of the Spirit, making the most of every opportunity. Then, he ends the section giving instructions for our homes.

Ephesians 5:21-33 and 6:1-4 are not necessarily a step-by-step manual with exact guidelines to leading a healthy home, but it is chock-full of principles, that if followed, will help us take responsibility for the authority we've been given. Specifically, Paul gives us some principles in Ephesians 5 and 6 for our marriage and our parenting. So, let's start with the first.

Part 1: Taking responsibility in my marriage

If we want to be the leader of our home, then our first leadership responsibility is to lead the way in submission.

I understand that not everyone who is reading this is married or even has the intention of being married. Some of you are divorced or widowed. Some might be called by God to singleness. Whatever the case, I believe these principles are good for all of us to know and understand.

You never know what people you might walk with in this life, counsel, pray for, or encourage, who are married or will be married. Just knowing these principles for marriage can help make you a better friend to those who are married. And honestly, they are just good principles to live by in any relationship.

Relationships are complicated. Marriage is hard. Regardless of what the fairytales tell us, and no matter what the movies portray, happily ever after isn't real. Happy, healthy, fulfilling, intimate, and lifelong marriages do exist, but they aren't easy. It's hard work.

You don't just find the "right person," and then everything works out. It starts by becoming the right person, pursing the right things, and leading the right way before you ever develop a thriving marriage. Isn't that what we all long for in marriage, a thriving one? I don't know about you, but I don't just want a marriage that lasts, I want a marriage that is alive! I want a marriage that thrives.

Some of us have already dropped the ball here, right? We've made choices in our relationships that have wreaked havoc in our lives. For you, a thriving marriage might be a distant memory or a desperate dream. So, let me encourage us again with these words:

Regardless of what you've done or gone through. Whether you are married, single, divorced, or widowed. No matter who you are or where you've been; happy, healthy, holy, and whole is God's dream for you, and it's never too late to start pursuing that dream.

There is no sin God can't forgive, no relationship He can't heal, and no pit He can't pull you out of. He is a God of mercy, grace, forgiveness and redemption. He is for you, not against you, and He will do whatever it takes to see you win in your home. With that said, how do we start taking responsibility in our marriages?

I believe it all starts with submission. I need to submit myself! You might ask, "Submit myself to what?" While that's a great question, I think a better question would be, "Submit myself to whom?"

In Ephesians chapter 5, we often start our teaching on marriage with the women. We say things like, "Well, the Bible says that husbands should lead, and wives should submit to their husbands. So, she should submit to me!" That's when the metaphorical nuclear bomb explodes, right? I don't know of a more divisive word in our marriage teaching than submit, especially when it comes to women. The Bible does say that by the way.

Ephesians 5:22-24 For wives, this means submit to your husband as to the Lord. ²³ For a husband is the head of his wife as Christ is the head of the Church. He is the Savior of his body, the Church. ²⁴ As the Church submits to Christ, so you wives should submit to your husbands in everything.

As men, we're great at emphasizing the word "submit," aren't we? That one word, "submit," has not only been misunderstood in the Church, but it has been misused and abused as well.

Many times, we use that word to try and control or manipulate our spouse. We bring it up when we aren't getting our way or we're losing an argument. Like me getting off that ski lift, our use of the word "submit" has caused chaos and wreaked havoc in our homes.

So, let me ask this question. Did you know that husbands are supposed to submit as well? Guys, for us to say that husbands lead, and wives submit is not revealing the whole truth. We often jump to verse 22 of Ephesians chapter 5 without even mentioning the verse before.

Ephesians 5:21 **²¹And further, submit to one another out of reverence for Christ.**

Men, if we want to be the leader of our home, then our first leadership responsibility is to lead the way in submission. We should not only learn, but also live out four words that everyone needs to know. These four words, if lived out, would change every relationship in our life for the better. Are you ready for the words? Here they are: "It's not about me!" Say it out loud if you need to, "It's not about me!"

MEN, IF WE WANT TO BE THE LEADER OF OUR HOME, THEN OUR FIRST LEADERSHIP RESPONSIBILITY IS TO LEAD THE WAY IN SUBMISSION.

That's just good advice for all relationships whether you believe in Jesus or not. The Bible is full of principles, that whether you believe in God or follow Jesus, they are still true, helpful, and applicable to our lives.

For instance, **"Do unto others as you would want them to do unto you."** (Matthew 7:12) You don't have to be a Christian to know, that's just a good principle to live by.

"It's more blessed to give than to receive." (Acts 20:35) You don't have to know God to know that generosity is better than greed.

That's just two, out of dozens of principles, that whether you believe in Jesus or not will bring the teachings of Jesus to the center of your life and will make your life better. The same is true with marriage.

Submission is one of those principles. Submission won't make your marriage perfect, but as you begin to live out those four words, "it's not about me," you will start to see your pursuits in marriage and purpose for marriage change.

"Submit to one another," we're told. For followers of Jesus though, it goes one step deeper. "Out of reverence for Christ!" Here, Paul is telling us that our reverence for Christ should drive everything we do in all our relationships, including marriage. Woah!

Think about that statement. "Is everything I'm doing in my relationships bringing reverence to Christ?" That will stop many of the things we choose to do dead in their tracks. Yes, those things you're thinking of right now. This means, not only should submission be at the center of our relationships (marriage), but Jesus needs to be at the center of our submission. Let that sink in.

Now, I'll be the first to acknowledge, you can have a happy and healthy marriage without Jesus. It can be done. I just think the odds are greatly diminished. If Jesus is not at the center of the marriage, then submission will not be sought after in the marriage.

> **IF JESUS IS NOT AT THE CENTER OF THE MARRIAGE, THEN SUBMISSION WILL NOT BE SOUGHT AFTER IN THE MARRIAGE.**

I believe the first pursuit in marriage should be submission and the sole purpose of marriage is reverence for Christ. Everything else flows from there. So, how do I submit to my wife out of reverence for Christ?

Ephesians 5:25 [25] **For husbands, this means love your wives, just as Christ loved the Church. He gave up his life for her** [26] **to make her holy and clean, washed by the cleansing of God's word.**

That's it guys! Love. That's how we rise-up and take responsibility in our marriage. That's how we pursue submission to our wives out of reverence for Christ.

Now, the three acts of love I'm proposing aren't the only things a husband should do for his wife, but if we focus on these three things it will be a great start to keeping the right pursuits and having the right purpose in our marriage.

The first way Jesus loved the Church, and the first way we should submissively love our wives is to seek them.

Luke 19:10 - For the Son of Man came to seek and save those who are lost.

This is hard for us as men. We are typically hunters by nature. Think about hunting for a moment. I personally don't enjoy hunting, but this illustration fits well in my own life.

A hunter typically has the ideal picture in mind of what they'd like to harvest, right? If I said, "Describe the perfect deer." A lot of men would go into pretty specific detail about the kind of deer they'd like to bag.

When you go hunting, you cover up who you are with camouflage, put on a scent to attract the animal, make the right sounds or keep from certain sounds to draw in the animal. Then, after tracking them down and getting them in your sights, you pull out your weapon, take your shot, pose for a picture with what you've bagged, and the pursuit is over.

If you think about it, I just described flirting, dating, engagement, and the wedding for so many men.

Before marriage, if I asked a guy to describe the perfect spouse, he would be able to give specific details about the kind of woman he would love to marry. From their looks to their lifestyle he would get specific. In his pursuit of this perfect catch, he covers up who he really is, puts on a scent to attract her, and uses or avoids certain words and sounds to draw her in.

After tracking her down and having her in his sights, he pulls out the weapon. This time, instead of a rifle it's a ring. They get engaged, tie the knot, pose for a picture, and the pursuit stops. It's a funny analogy, but it's so true.

When it comes to marriage, once we "catch" what we're after, we oftentimes don't continue the pursuit. Husbands, we need to seek our wives. I don't know what that looks like for you. I don't know your wife like you do. I could make suggestions, but that's about it. All I know is, for you to take responsibility in your marriage, you need to seek your wife.

Here's why this is so important. If you stop seeking your wife, an opportunity will arise for her to be pursued by someone else. Deep down, I believe every woman wants to be sought by a man. Cherished. Adored. Protected. Pursued. Yes, even led!

YOUR WIFE IS NOT JUST SOMEONE YOU DID PURSUE, SHE IS THE ONE PERSON TO KEEP PURSUING!

Husbands, physically speaking, you are the only acceptable option of fulfilling that need in your wife's heart. Everything else will lead her away from you, and most likely away from the Lord.

By the way ladies, this is why your first pursuit must be Jesus. If you are not being filled and fulfilled in Christ, then when you are not being pursued by a man, you'll be tempted to compromise your values to feel valued. Your value comes from Christ alone!

Husbands seek your wives. Date them. Get away for a weekend. Ask them questions. Surprise them. Write notes to them. Do what you did before you were married so that you never lose the connection after you're married. Your wife is not just someone you did pursue, she is the one person to keep pursuing!

The second way we submissively love our wives like Christ loved us is to serve them.

Mark 10:45 [45] **For even the Son of Man came not to be served but to serve others and to give his life as a ransom for many.**

The best way I've found to live this out is to learn what my wife hates to do around the house, and then start doing that for her. By the way, it's a whole lot easier to discover this if you are also determined to seek your wife.

Ask your wife, "What am I currently not doing that you'd like me to start doing for you?" Then after she picks her jaw up from the floor and tells you, start doing it. Don't wait for her to ask the same question. Don't argue about what she doesn't do for you. Remember, "it's not about me!" The opportunities to serve your wife are literally endless.

Figure out what your wife's love language is and do it. My wife calls this, "Filling your spouse's love bucket." If you don't know what her love language is, start there.

> IF YOU DON'T SERVE YOUR WIFE, THEN YOU DON'T LOVE HER LIKE JESUS LOVED YOU.

In his book "*The 5 Love Languages*", Gary Chapman spells it out. Do a web search for, "*The 5 Love Languages*", and you'll probably find an online test that will reveal your love languages in a matter of minutes.[1] There is even a 5 Love Languages app that will provide all the resources you need.

To give you a head start, there are five basic love languages, or ways that each person receives and gives love the best. The way you best receive love might be different than the way you best give it. Most likely, the way your spouse receives and gives love is totally different than yours.

The five languages are: Words of affirmation, acts of service, receiving gifts, quality time, and physical touch. Notice, the last one is not sex, but physical touch. You may not believe it, but there is a big difference!

So, start there. Find out her love language and fill it. Even if it's not the way you like to receive or give love yourself. Isn't that how Jesus loved you? If you don't serve your wife, then you don't love her like Jesus loved you.

The last way we submissively love our wives like Christ loved us to spoil them. Before you get too excited ladies, I'm talking about way more than just spending more money on you.

1 John 3:1 See what great love the Father has lavished on us, that we should be called children of God!

You might be thinking, "Why in the world should I spoil her when she hasn't earned it from me?"

I understand there are men reading this book who aren't in a healthy marriage relationship. Some of you have a wife who is not currently on board or holding up her end of the covenant you made between each other and God. I understand that, but that's all the more reason you become like Christ when you seek, serve, and spoil her.

Psalm 103:10 - He (God) does not punish us for all our sins; he does not deal harshly with us, as we deserve.

Spoiling your wife means treating her the way God expects, not the way she has earned. Ouch! Guys let me challenge you with something. What if each day we assumed our wife was unsure we still loved her, then we set out that day to prove to her that we do?

> SPOILING YOUR WIFE MEANS TREATING HER THE WAY GOD EXPECTS, NOT THE WAY SHE HAS EARNED.

I want to treat my wife in such a way that the only thing which would ever cause her to look for physical or relational fulfillment elsewhere would be my death. Even then, I hope I have raised the bar so high that only God's best in a man could match my love for her.

We don't demand submission, we demonstrate it through our love. The kind of love Jesus demonstrated for us means He doesn't have to demand submission, we willingly want to submit to the kind of love Jesus shows. The same is true in marriage.

I've added an entire section for the wives in Appendix 4, so I won't belabor the point here. I do want to say this to all the ladies who have come this far, and to the men as well. The word "submit" that is used here in Ephesians means, *"I place under, become subject to; I put myself under someone's authority."* [2] That's important to understand.

Submission in marriage is a choice not a condition. Wives, you are not less than your husband when you submit, and men, you are not less than your wife when you submit. The whole point is, we are all less than Christ, and He should be at the center of our marriage. It's out of reverence for Him that I choose to submit.

Men, whether we realize it or not we are a leader and we are all leading somewhere. So, I challenge you to lead your wife to Jesus! Make Jesus your first priority, submission your first pursuit and the right purpose will naturally follow.

I can say I'm "the leader" all I want, but until I make Jesus my first pursuit and submission my first priority, I'm just riding up the ski lift toward an oncoming disaster. Until I seek, serve and spoil my wife; doing my best to lead her towards Jesus and helping her fulfill her dreams and calling in Him, I'm just flailing my arms, kicking my ski's, and knocking people down.

Because God has given me authority in my marriage, I will rise-up and take responsibility by making Jesus my first pursuit and submission my first priority. I will lead the way in submission by seeking, serving, and spoiling my wife, leading her with the same love that Jesus has shown me.

This is my declaration!

Part 2: Taking responsibility in my parenting

Success as a parent is not found in obedience or outcomes, but in offering them my best.

I believe parenting is God's way of showing us how desperately we need Him. Without question, parenting is the most difficult thing I've ever done in my life. At the same time, it has brought me the most joy!

I can't think of anything else in my life that makes me laugh more, smile bigger, or make me prouder than my kids. Seeing them change and grow into amazing young men and women is the greatest part of my life.

My children are a blessing from God. They don't always feel like a blessing, but they are. Even in times of great burden as a parent I cannot believe that God loaned these four souls to our care. The fact that God has entrusted us with them is an incredible weight to bear, and if I'm honest, more often than not I feel like a failure as a parent. I struggle with that.

That's where this chapter comes from. It comes from seventeen years of lessons. In no way am I the one to be writing a "how to" chapter on parenting. I know many of you have way more years under your belt as a parent, and much more expertise. So, I'm not writing this from a place of authority on the subject, but a place of humility and surrender.

Like the section on marriage, I know some of you may not currently be a parent. While you may not be a parent now, at the very least, you have had or do have parents. You are friends with people who are parents. You work with parents. Maybe God can use this part of the book to give you a new perspective of your own parents, or a new way to pray for and walk with people in your life who are parents.

I want to be very clear, I love every one of my kids. My biggest fear in sharing this portion of the book is projecting something onto them from my own struggles or shortcomings. This is not about the behavior of my children, it's about the burden every parent has to bear.

This is about the responsibility we have as dads to rise-up, take responsibility, lead our children well, modeling the life we desire for them to live. No matter how you've led as a dad in the past or how you're leading now, today is the start of a new day! Today we will begin to take responsibility in our parenting.

I can't imagine my life without my kids. I *can* imagine one solid week without 'em, can I get a witness for that? I can't imagine though, my life without my kids. I love them. I love them unconditionally. There is nothing my kids can do to make me love them less and nothing they can do to make me love them more. While I love my kids, I don't always love the way I parent them.

Before you have kids, you think you'll be the perfect parent, right? You see kids acting up in public and think, "My kids will never do that!" Or, "When I'm a parent...," and you fill in the blank with brilliant advice to yourself. "If they would just do this or do that, then their kids wouldn't act that way."

Then God blesses you with kids and you realize, you don't know jack squat! So now, when I see parents dealing with an out of control kid at the store, I just nod with the, "I know exactly how you feel," look. I've been there when my kid was rolling on the floor in the middle of the aisle. I know how embarrassing that is.

I've had my share of moments where I throw my hands up in despair, not knowing what to do next. I go to bed sometimes and think, "I shouldn't have said that to them." Or, "I shouldn't have said it that way." "I should have been more involved here, spent a little more time there, said yes to them there."

We spend lots of time second guessing ourselves as parents, don't we? There are times as a parent, and I'm not sure this ever goes away, where your kids behave a certain way and you immediately feel like you did something wrong. "Where did I go wrong as a parent? Where did I fail?"

This is where we've got to be very careful that we don't take the blame for our kids' mistakes. This is so important to understand. If I take the blame for my kids' mistakes, I'll just as quickly take the credit for their successes. When I do that, I have taken the place of God in their life. If their mistakes are my fault and their successes are from my strength, then neither they nor I need God.

> IF I TAKE THE BLAME FOR MY KIDS' MISTAKES, I'LL JUST AS QUICKLY TAKE THE CREDIT FOR THEIR SUCCESSES.

The truth is though, even on my best days, I still fall desperately short of what my kids need. Even at my best, I make mistakes and need to ask for forgiveness. Which by the way, one of the best things you can do for your kids is admit when you're wrong and ask for their forgiveness. That might be the one thing someone needed to get out of this chapter.

Even at my best, I can't do everything for my kids. I can't control the outcome of their life or make them obey. This might seem like the most discouraging talk on parenting you've ever heard, but it's actually right where we need to be in order to receive the truth God wants us to hear.

You see, as parents, more often than not, we are truly doing our best or what we believe is best at the time. Yes, there are some parents who completely disregard their responsibility as caregiver to a child, and some of you have been on the receiving end of that, but the vast majority of parents really are doing their best. Yet, even in our best, we beat ourselves up over what we didn't do or what our kids didn't do that they should have, and we feel like a failure all over again.

That's why, to rise-up and take responsibility in our parenting, we have to remember this principle: As parents, success is not found in obedience or outcomes, it's found in offering them my best.

Because my best still falls short though, there must be something else I need. So, what else do I need in my parenting? This is not a practical look at parenting but some principles I see in Scripture that can bridge the gap between my best and what my kids need.

These principles remain true no matter how old your kids are, how they have lived or currently are living, or how you've parented them in the past. For those of you who aren't parents, this is how you can be praying for those of us who are, encouraging us to seek this out in our lives.

Many of us are familiar with the story of Samson in the Bible. Most people, even those of us who have rarely gone to Church at least know parts of his story. Samson was set apart by God and given supernatural strength beyond our human understanding. As much as he is known for his feats of strength though, he is also known for his failures.

Samson had many weaknesses, the last being his love for a Philistine woman named Delilah. The Philistines were the enemy of God's people, Israel. Delilah was approached and paid by them to learn the source of Samson's strength.

Following several failed attempts, Delilah finally seduces the secret of his strength from him. He confesses, "If you cut off my hair I will be like any other man." (Judges 16:17) After lulling him to sleep, most likely using the effects of alcohol to do so, she cut off his hair, called in the enemy soldiers with whom she was working, and we're told:

Judges 16:20-21 [20] Then she cried out, "Samson! The Philistines have come to capture you!" When he woke up, he thought, "I will do as before and shake myself free." But he didn't realize the Lord had left him. [21] So the Philistines captured him and gouged out his eyes. They took him to Gaza, where he was bound with bronze chains and forced to grind grain in the prison.

Now if that was the only part of the story you knew you might wonder, "What kind of parents did this dude have?" You wouldn't guess this as the ending to someone's story who came from parents who gave their best, right? I mean, this young man obviously came from a home where he was not taught the ways of the Lord or given a Godly example to follow.

So, what kind of parents did Samson have? Perhaps the story of Samson's parents can help us be encouraged in our own parenting. I'm sure Samson didn't turn out the way his parents hoped. When he was born, I doubt their dream for him was to abandon God, reveal the secret of his Divine strength to a "lady of the night," and have his eyes gouged out by the enemy of God's people.

When God revealed this to me personally it helped me so much in my own parenting. The outcome of Samson's life was not the fault of the way he was parented. Remember, as parents, success is not determined by outcomes or obedience, but in offering them our best, and since our best still falls short, what else do we need in our parenting?

Judges 13:1-8; 12 **¹ Again the Israelites did evil in the Lord's sight, so the Lord handed them over to the Philistines, who oppressed them for forty years. ² In those days a man named Manoah from the tribe of Dan lived in the town of Zorah. His wife was unable to become pregnant, and they had no children. ³ The angel of the Lord appeared to Manoah's wife and said, "Even though you have been unable to have children, you will soon become pregnant and give birth to a son. ⁴ So be careful; you must not drink wine or any other alcoholic drink nor eat any forbidden food. ⁵ You will become pregnant and give birth to a son, and his hair must never be cut. For he will be dedicated to God as a Nazirite from birth.** (A Nazarite was set apart to serve God for a specific purpose, and they were under a vow to not touch any alcoholic drink, forbidden food, a dead body, or to cut their own hair.) **He will begin to rescue Israel from the Philistines." ⁶ The woman ran and told her husband, "A man of God appeared to me! He looked like one of God's angels, terrifying to see. I didn't ask**

> ... AS PARENTS, SUCCESS IS NOT DETERMINED BY OUTCOMES OR OBEDIENCE, BUT IN OFFERING THEM OUR BEST, ...

where he was from, and he didn't tell me his name. [7] But he told me, 'You will become pregnant and give birth to a son. You must not drink wine or any other alcoholic drink nor eat any forbidden food. For your son will be dedicated to God as a Nazirite from the moment of his birth until the day of his death.'" [8] Then Manoah prayed to the Lord, saying, "Lord, please let the man of God come back to us again and give us more instructions about this son who is to be born." (God answered their prayer, and the angel came back.) [12] So Manoah asked him, "When your words come true, what kind of rules should govern the boy's life and work?"

If we are to rise-up as men and take responsibility in our parenting, then the first thing I see in Manoah that we desperately need is this: We need to seek God's counsel.

It stood out to me that Manoah prayed for *more* instructions, and when the angel returned he went on to ask, "What kind of rules should govern the boy's life and work?"

If I'm ever going to bridge the gap between my best and what my kids really need, I better be asking God the same questions. "What kind of rules should govern my child's life and work? What do I need to be teaching them? What should I be modeling for them? What should I be praying over them? What promises should I be claiming on their behalf?"

Look at what God tells fathers through the Apostle Paul in his letter to the Ephesians:

Ephesians 6:4 [4] **Fathers, do not provoke your children to anger by the way you treat them. Rather, bring them up with the discipline and instruction that comes from the Lord.**

The word discipline does not mean punishment, it means training. Am I bringing my children up with the training and instruction that comes from the Lord? Am I laying before my kids the pathway to real life? Am I calling my children to a life of holiness while also consistently modeling it for them?

Manoah knew his best wasn't enough. Samson needed something more, so he sought the counsel of God. Men, nothing should drive us to our knees in prayer or lead us to the Word of God more than our own kids. We can't do this on our own. My best is not good enough. My strength isn't strong enough. My wisdom isn't wise enough.

Just like Manoah, when we cry out to God for help He will be there to answer us. His answer may not be in the form of our child's perfect obedience or the outcome we prefer for their life, but in His overwhelming grace and strength to lead them well.

I have no doubt that Manoah continued seeking God's counsel in his parenting. This wasn't a one-time request. I believe he brought up Samson with the training and instruction that comes from the Lord, doing his best to rely on the Lord. And this never ends.

I'm 44 years old and I know my parents still seek God's counsel on my behalf. They may not have the same authority in my life today, but they still understand their responsibility to speak training into my life as their son. Our responsibility never ends and it's never too late to begin.

Samson, like all of us, had a free will. In spite of how great a father he had in Manoah, he still chose to walk away from the Lord. That leads right into the next thing I think we need in our parenting. After we seek God's counsel, we also need to surrender control.

Judges 14:1-4 [1] One day when Samson was in Timnah, one of the Philistine women caught his eye. [2] When he returned home, he told his father and mother, "A young Philistine woman in Timnah caught my eye. I want to marry her. Get her for me." [3] His father and mother objected. "Isn't there even one woman in our tribe or among all the Israelites you could marry?" they asked. "Why must you go to the pagan Philistines to find a wife?" (Can't you just feel their parental anxiety? "Samson, this is not how we raised you." "God, I thought we raised him correctly? Where did we go wrong? Where did we fail as parents?") **But Samson told his father, "Get her for me! She looks good to me." [4] His father**

and mother didn't realize the Lord was at work in this, creating an opportunity to work against the Philistines, who ruled over Israel at that time.

> GOD DOES NOT CAUSE OUR KIDS TO DO EVIL, BUT HE CAN USE THEIR EVIL TO WORK FOR HIS CAUSE.

The last verse is so amazing and encouraging for me as a parent. For Samson, even in going against the way he was raised, the Lord was still moving in it, creating an opportunity to work against the Philistines. Don't forget, this was the original purpose God had designed for Samson, to rescue the people of Israel from the Philistines.

Now, the Bible doesn't say this, so please understand this is my opinion of Scripture. As I read this, based on the kind of people his parents already revealed themselves to be, I assume they had also come to a place where they surrendered Samson to God's control. They didn't agree with what Samson was doing. They definitely did not support his lifestyle, but they had surrendered to God's control.

Here is a truth that I'm still learning to understand, and I see it here in the story of Samson. God does not cause our kids to do evil, but He can use their evil to work for His cause. His parents didn't realize it at the time, but God was using Samson's defiance to bring glory to Himself. Did you know that's actually a principle from the Bible?

Psalm 76:10 Human defiance only enhances your glory, for you use it as a weapon.

We don't always see the big picture. We can't see what God is allowing in our kids' lives or doing behind the scenes that leads to His glory in the end.

Just recently, I found myself in a parenting wrestling match with God. Some things weren't happening the way I thought they should for one of our kids and I was reminding God of that fact. I've learned that whenever I try to remind God about something, He usually reminds me of exactly who's in charge.

I could take you to the spot on the road where I was driving in my truck, letting God know how much I loved my kids, how I wanted the best for them, and how He wasn't doing what I wanted in their life. It was in that moment that I felt the gracious, yet serious voice of God say, "Jeff, do you love them more than I do?" That stopped me dead in my complaining tracks. "I know you love your kids Jeff, but I actually died for them. I think I've got this. Do you trust me with your kids or not?"

That was a watershed moment for me. Driving down the road I surrendered control. "God, I'm sorry for trying to control the outcome of my children. I repent for not trusting You. Please forgive me. I know that You love them more than I do, and You won't abandon Your plan for their life. I surrender control to You!" The only thing that could have made the moment more powerful would have been if *"Jesus Take The Wheel"* started playing on the radio.[1]

Now, this hasn't made parenting any easier and I've had to repent on more than one occasion since then for trying to regain control, but I keep going back to that moment. God loves my kids more than I do. He is in control. I've got to trust Him through surrender.

After the first part of Judges 14, we don't see or hear from Samson's parents again. Where were they? In all of chapter 13, they were the focus. Up through the wedding in chapter 14 they were at least a part of Samson's story. Now they're gone. It appears that they are no longer a part of his story, and this is where his story goes off the rails.

Between the last part of chapter 14 through the first part of chapter 16, here's a few things that happen: Samson ripped a lion's jaw apart with his bare hands. He called his fiancé a "heifer". At one point, he killed thirty men and took their belongings to pay off a debt he owed. His fiancé then married someone else (big surprise), so in his anger he caught 300 foxes, tied them together in pairs by the tails, fastened a torch to each pair, lit the torches on fire and set them loose in the grain fields nearby, burning them to the ground.

As if that isn't crazy enough, he killed more Philistines, allowed 3,000 men to capture and tie him up with ropes, only to rip himself free from the ropes killing 1,000 of those men with the jawbone of a dead donkey. He hired a prostitute, which doesn't go well, so he ripped the gate of the city off its hinges and carried it away. Then, everything comes to a crashing halt in his relationship with Delilah.

As mentioned before, she seduces him, and cuts off his hair thus causing his strength to leave. He was then captured by the Philistines, his eyes were gouged out, he was chained as a slave to a millstone where he would push it around in circles day after day.

This is not where Samson's parents thought their child, this gift from God, an answer to their prayers of infertility, would end up. Did they feel like a failure? Did they blame themselves? I don't know. All I know is this, while Samson was pushing a grindstone God was allowing him to regain his strength.

Judges 16:22 ²² But before long, his hair began to grow back.

Remember, Samson's strength was in his hair and his hair began to grow back. In other words, God wasn't done yet! The story of Samson and his parents had not yet been completed, and your story hasn't either.

The Philistines eventually threw a big party to worship their pagan god Dagon. They brought Samson out to taunt him and to celebrate the defeat of God's "chosen" people. As Samson stood there, he asked the servants to put his hands on the pillars that support the temple. The temple was completely filled for the party. All the Philistine rulers were there with 3,000 people watching on the roof. In that moment we are told, **"Then Samson prayed."** (Judges 16:28)

Don't let that slip by. That one statement, **"Then Samson prayed,"** is so powerful. Perhaps it was in hitting rock bottom that caused Samson to look up to God. Maybe, while pushing the grindstone, God reminded him of his purpose. Could it be that he remembered the things his parents said, did, and told him when he was a child?

I don't know what was going through his mind in that moment, all I know is what he prayed: **"Sovereign Lord, remember me again. O God, please strengthen me just one more time. With one blow let me pay back the Philistines for the loss of my two eyes."** **(Judges 16:28)**

Samson put his hands on the pillars, knocked down the temple, killing more people in that one moment than during his entire lifetime. In the last moment *of* his life he fulfilled God's purpose *for* his life, rescuing Israel from the Philistines.

By the time of Samson's death his parents had already passed away. We don't know when they died, but while their physical bodies had been buried, their prayers had not. Their prayers were fully alive, and they were answered in that final moment.

Perhaps somewhere in a private home, far away from the grindstone, a father was on his knees in prayer. If alive, the news of Samson's capture would have only compounded the pain, heartache, and tears in their life. The feeling of being a failure would have been rising in full force.

But maybe, just maybe, in a moment of prayer, Manoah was reminded of the promise of God for his child. Perhaps in the midst of his pain, he again cried out for the counsel of God, continued surrendering to the control of God, and stood on the faithful commitment of God.

UNTIL SAMSON'S FINAL BREATH, GOD WAS PURSUING HIM, AND UNTIL YOUR CHILD'S FINAL BREATH, HE WILL PURSUE THEM AS WELL.

Until Samson's final breath, God was pursuing him, and until your child's final breath He will pursue them as well. We have got to stand on God's faithful commitment toward our children.

Success as a parent is not found in obedience or outcomes, but in offering them my best. My best though, still falls dreadfully short of what they need. So, I will rise-up and take responsibility as a father, offering them my best by seeking God's counsel for them, surrendering my control of them, and standing on God's commitment to them.

This is my declaration!

EIGHT

HONOR GOD FINANCIALLY

Honoring God with our finances is not a burden for us to bear, it's a blessing for us to live.

Perspective changes everything, right? A couple years ago now, I ended my day at the office like I often do by going out for a run. I have a particular route I like to run that loops out from our Church, goes about 3.5 miles total, and ends back at the Church.

On this day, I was maybe a half a mile from the Church, running down one of the main roads in our community, when I saw who I thought was Jared, our worship pastor, driving towards me on the road. In the moment, it didn't even cross my mind that it could be someone else.

At the time, Jared drove a car that I didn't think many people in town drove. Not because it was so nice, quite the opposite. At the time, he drove a 1996, sun faded green, Subaru Legacy. Nothing against a Subaru Legacy, but this car was in the final days of its legacy, if you know what I mean.

So, I'm running down the road, Jared is driving towards me, and I change my normal running motion into something you'd see from a lanky 6th grade boy on a basketball court. You know what I'm talking about, right? Their legs and arms are flailing because their body has outgrown their coordination skills. So, while I'm running in the most obnoxious way I can, I'm also giving this giant goofy grin, and waving like a mad-man. All I wanted to do was get a laugh out of my worship pastor.

That's when I realized, this is either not Jared, or Jared has really changed in the last hour since I saw him. This guy was leaned back in his seat as if he was riding in a tricked-out sports car. He had a tattered t-shirt on, unkempt hair, and not only did he look nothing like Jared, but he had a long cigarette just hanging out of his mouth.

Needless to say, I immediately stopped acting like a moron, stared straight at the ground and thought, "I just gave that guy the story of his week, and now I have an illustration as well."

Perspective changes everything. My point of view determined my priority in the moment and the practice in my life.

I believe, when it comes to God and money, we need a massive perspective shift. Money is such a divisive subject, especially in the Church. I'm going to hold you to a higher expectation, though. I believe, if you've read this far, you're going to keep reading, even if we're talking about money.

So far, we've talked about some pretty sensitive subjects. We've talked about the pain of our past and overcoming impurity to pursue the purity God expects of us. We've talked about taking responsibility in marriage, parenting, and all of our relationships. So, if we can talk through and overcome those, then we can get through this.

Just like my run, the closer you get to something the better you can see and understand it. The same is true with money. So often, we think God's out to get something from us. If that's our understanding about money, then our perspective is off.

So, before we go any further in our discussion about money, I want you to know that neither I nor God want to just get something from you, we want something for you as well. God wants you to live in the fullness of life that Jesus died to provide. He wants you to live in the flow of His abundant blessing that pours out on those who surrender to Him.

Honoring God with our finances is not a burden for us to bear, it's a blessing for us to live. That my friend is a perspective shift. If trying to honor God is a burden, we're not doing it right. We don't understand it fully.

Acts 20:35b You should remember the words of the Lord Jesus: "It is more blessed to give than to receive."

If I were to ask, "How many of us want to live in the blessing of God?" we would all raise our hands, right? Everyone wants to live in God's blessing. Even God wants us to live in His blessing, and He provides the guidelines to get there as well. It just takes a perspective shift about money.

> HONORING GOD WITH OUR FINANCES IS NOT A BURDEN FOR US TO BEAR, IT'S A BLESSING FOR US TO LIVE.

In the first seven chapters of Genesis, I believe God gives us insight into nearly every aspect of what it means to live in Biblical manhood. In those chapters there is truth about purity, taking responsibility, purpose, leadership and yes, money!

If you know your Bible, you might be racking your brain trying to think of a money story in the first part of Genesis. While nothing is specifically said about money, the principles about money are there.

We're going to see four principles about money that can help us rise-up, change our perspective, and set us on a course to honor God financially. Remember, honoring God financially is not a burden for us to bear, but a blessing for us to live in.

In Genesis 2:15 we see the very first principle about money. This principle has the power to set so many people free. I believe, more than anything, when we get the right perspective on this one thing, everything else will fall into place.

Genesis 2:15 ¹⁵ The LORD God placed the man (mankind) **in the Garden of Eden to tend and watch over it.**

It was God who made the Garden, and it was mankind that was commissioned to manage it. This is the key to the whole subject of money, and the foundation for every area of my life. It's only three words, and here they are. It's not mine!

The first one and a half chapters of Genesis are all about God creating this amazing place in which we live. Everything we see, have, are, and experience was created by God. Did anyone help God? No! Not one person. You and I definitely didn't help Him, and neither did Adam or Eve.

After creating this spectacular planet, and a garden that had to be more majestic than anything we've ever laid eyes on, God placed Adam and Eve into His creation to tend and watch over it. The garden didn't belong to them, but they were blessed by it, and were charged with managing it. That's a truth about money as well. It doesn't belong to me. It's not mine. This reality is repeated over and over again in Scripture.

Psalm 24:1 The earth is the Lord's, and *everything* in it. The world and all its people belong to him. (emphasis added)

King David even recognized this when He was raising money to build the Temple of God. David was challenging himself and all the people of Israel to give sacrificially, and generously to the building of God's house. In the midst of his challenge, he lifted up this prayer to His God.

1 Chronicles 29:11-14 [11] **Yours, O Lord, is the greatness, the power, the glory, the victory, and the majesty. *Everything* in the heavens and on earth is yours, O Lord, and this is your kingdom. We adore you as the one who is over all things.** [12] **Wealth and honor come from you alone, for you rule over everything. Power and might are in your hand, and at your discretion people are made great and given strength.** [13] **"O our God, we thank you and praise your glorious name!** [14] **But who am I, and who are my people, that we could give anything to you? *Everything* we have has come from you, and we give you only what you first gave us!** (emphasis added)

Wow! Did you see all that? It's not mine. We aren't owners, we're managers. Even when I give, I'm not really giving God something as if He should be impressed, I'm just returning what is already His.

You see, God might be pleased with our giving, but He's never impressed. You could give God your entire paycheck every time you got paid and it would never blow God away. You wouldn't be doing Him any favors. Why? It's all His to begin with.

Until we understand that money isn't ours, we'll never live in the blessing of being given any of it in the first place.

In the first two chapters of Genesis, God sets the precedent for everything in life. "I am the owner; you are the managers." Or speaking for ourselves, "It's not mine."

So, when it comes to our lives, bodies, relationships, possessions, and even our money, we are managers not owners. None of it belongs to me but all of it can be a blessing to me if I live according to the principles of God.

Fast forward in the Genesis story and we'll see that Adam and Eve have eaten the forbidden fruit, sin enters the world, creation is corrupted, and the very first family has been started. Eve bears two sons, Cain and Abel. It's in their story that we see the remaining three principles about money.

UNTIL WE UNDERSTAND THAT MONEY ISN'T OURS, WE'LL NEVER LIVE IN THE BLESSING OF BEING GIVEN ANY OF IT IN THE FIRST PLACE.

Genesis 4:1-7 ¹ Now Adam had sexual relations with his wife, Eve, and she became pregnant. When she gave birth to Cain, she said, "With the LORD's help, I have produced a man!" ² Later she gave birth to his brother and named him Abel. When they grew up, Abel became a shepherd, while Cain cultivated the ground. ³ When it was time for the harvest (or in our terminology, "payday".)**, Cain presented some of his crops as a gift to the LORD. ⁴ Abel also brought a gift—the best of the**

firstborn lambs from his flock. The LORD accepted Abel and his gift, [5] but he did not accept Cain and his gift. This made Cain very angry, and he looked dejected. [6] "Why are you so angry?" the LORD asked Cain. "Why do you look so dejected? [7] You will be accepted if you do what is right.

Don't miss this. There is so much power and so much potential for how this story can impact our lives. God said to Cain, **"You will be accepted if you do what is right."**

In this specific scenario, what was "right" that Cain had not done? Giving God the first and the best of his "payday." Abel gave the first and best of the lambs from his flock, but Cain gave some of his crops to the Lord.

This is another principle that runs all the way through Scripture. It's found here in Genesis chapter four, it weaves through the entire Old Testament, it is fulfilled in the sacrificial death and resurrection of Jesus, and it is lived out through the rest of the New Testament. This principle is the second thing we need to understand if we want to rise-up and honor God financially: God expects the first and the best of our income.

Why does God expect the first and the best? Which by the way, those aren't two different things when it comes to money? When it comes to money, the first *is* the best. In an agricultural and farming context this would have been different.

For instance, if the first lamb was lame, you wouldn't give it to God because it wouldn't be the best. If the first crops were diseased, you wouldn't give them to God because it wouldn't be the best. With money though, the first is the best. So, why does God expect the first?

The reason God expects the first is tied directly to the initial principle we discussed. It's His money, so He can ask for whatever He wants. Second, God knows that in giving Him the first, it is a sign that I trust Him and an act of worship to Him.

Proverbs 3:9 Honor (worship) **the LORD with your wealth and with the best part of everything you produce.**

So, if God expects the first and the best of our income to be given to Him, how do we do that in our current economical context? One word: Tithe!

The word tithe has five letters, but it may as well be a four-letter word in the Church. If you don't know, tithe means "tenth" or "ten percent". It represents the first 10% of all the income you earn through your labor being given back to God through the local Church you attend. This serves as a sign that you trust Him and a way you worship Him.

Malachi 3:8-10a says:

Malachi 3:8-10a [8] **"Should people cheat God? Yet you have cheated me! "But you ask, 'What do you mean? When did we ever cheat you?' "You have cheated me of the tithes and offerings due to me.** [9] **You are under a curse, for your whole nation has been cheating me.** [10] **Bring all the tithes into the storehouse** (Church) **so there will be enough food in my Temple.**

What I hear a lot from people in the Church is, "Well, that's from the Old Testament and is a part of the law. We're not under the law we're under grace. We live in the age of the New Testament where Jesus fulfilled the law, so the tithe is no longer expected by those of us who believe."

First of all, they're right about one thing. As Christians, we are no longer bound by the law. However, tithing is not a law, it's a principle throughout Scripture. You can't escape it. It was established before the law, continued in the law, and it was confirmed by Jesus after the law.

The principle of the first was established in Genesis 4 as we just read. In Genesis 14, hundreds of years before the law was even given, Abraham tithed to God through the High Priest Melchizedek. His tithe was a sign of trust in God and an act of worship to God.

In Genesis 28, still several hundred years before the law would be given, Jacob promises to give God a tenth of all he receives as a sign of his trust in God and a way to worship God. Then, not only are we commanded to tithe in the law, but Jesus confirms it through His teaching in the New Testament. In Matthew 23:23 Jesus says this to the Pharisees:

Matthew 23:23 What sorrow awaits you teachers of religious law and you Pharisees. Hypocrites! For you are careful to tithe even the tiniest income from your herb gardens, but you ignore the more important aspects of the law--justice, mercy, and faith. You should tithe, yes, but do not neglect the more important things.

At the very least, Jesus affirms the tithe as something we should be doing. I know there are many ways that people try and explain this teaching of Jesus away, so let me say it differently.

If we are living in the New Testament way of giving, I'd like you to show me one place in the New Testament where Jesus encourages anyone to live below what the law required. You won't find it.

Jesus took the law and elevated the expectation in our lives for everything. He took adultery and said, "If you even lust, you've already committed adultery in your heart." He took our enemies and said, "You shouldn't just love those who love you, you should love those who hate and mistreat you." He took murder and said, "If you hate someone, it's the same as murder." Jesus took nearly every Old Testament law and said, "Because the power of My Spirit now lives in you, I'm not excusing you to live below the law, I'm empowering you to live beyond it." (Matthew 5:21-48)

That's the New Testament reality of the law. The law is not something that burdens us in the New Testament, the law is something we are enabled to live beyond. Sadly, though, nearly every person I've ever talked to who claimed New Testament giving as their standard did so as an excuse to live below what the law required instead of being empowered to live beyond it.

God expects the first and the best. For Cain and Abel this happened at the "time of the harvest". For us it might be the fifteenth and thirtieth of the month. Maybe it's once a month, or every other week. Whatever "payday" is for you, that's when you honor God financially with the first and the best.

Cain offered "some" of his crops. In today's language we say, "Let me pay the bills first, fund my hobbies, experience some entertainment, and if I have any leftover then I'll give to God."

When we give to God from our leftovers what we're really saying is, "God, let me take care of all my needs first, then I'll honor You with what's left." Or, if we're being really honest, "God, I don't trust You to provide for all my needs."

THE LAW IS NOT SOMETHING THAT BURDENS US IN THE NEW TESTAMENT, THE LAW IS SOMETHING WE ARE ENABLED TO LIVE BEYOND.

Listen, I know this is an incredibly difficult step to take in life. I know that 10% is a large sum of money no matter how much you make. I know it seems like you can't afford to tithe right now. I would argue it's not that you can't afford to do it, you just don't have the right perspective towards money yet. It's amazing how much you can afford to do when you get the right perspective. It's not mine and God expects the first!

Now, you can't just give 10% and then blow the other 90% as if there's no tomorrow. One of the greatest benefits of giving away 10% of your income is it forces you to manage the other 90% well, and with the wisdom of God. You can't be loose with your spending if you give the first 10% away.

Yes, it's hard. Yes, it requires discipline. Yes, you'll make sacrifices, cut spending, give up some pleasures in life, and force yourself to live on a budget. That's all true, but so is this; God can do more with 90% than I can do with 100% on my own. And if I disobey this principle of tithing, that's what I am financially, on my own.

> ... THERE SHOULD BE A LEVEL OF DISCOMFORT IF YOU'RE KEEPING SOMETHING THAT BELONGS TO SOMEONE ELSE IN YOUR HOUSE, ESPECIALLY IF THAT SOMEONE ELSE IS THE PERSON WHO DIED IN YOUR PLACE!

If you need help in learning how to manage your money God's way, I cannot recommend strongly enough the resources of Joe Sangl. Joe is the founder of *"I Was Broke, Now I'm Not!"*, as well as the author of a book with the same name. There isn't any better resource out there to help you win with your money God's way than his. For more information, go to www.iwbnin.com.[1]

Listen, I've never seen someone truly surrender the tithe to God and regret it. I've never known someone who didn't experience the blessing of God in it. All I have belongs to God and He asks for the first and best in return. When I tithe, I'm revealing my attitude towards God. "All 100% belongs to You Lord, so here is the first 10% as a sign that I trust You and a way to worship You for providing in my life."

What's your attitude towards all this right now? How are you feeling? Listen, talking about this makes some of you uncomfortable doesn't it? The reality is, there should be a level of discomfort if you're keeping something that belongs to someone else in your house, especially if that someone else is the Person who died in your place!

This reveals the third principle about money we need to understand. My attitude towards money reflects my attitude towards God. God told Cain, "You'll be accepted if you do what is right." Then He says this:

Genesis 4:7b-10 But if you refuse to do what is right, then watch out! Sin is crouching at the door, eager to control you. But you must subdue it and be its master." [8] **One day Cain suggested to his brother, "Let's go out into the fields." And while they were in the field, Cain attacked his brother, Abel, and killed him.** [9] **Afterward the LORD asked Cain, "Where is your brother? Where is Abel?" "I don't know," Cain responded. "Am I my brother's**

guardian?" [10] But the LORD said, "What have you done? Listen! Your brother's blood cries out to me from the ground!

Listen, this is so huge. Don't just brush past this. Cain's disobedience financially led to the murder of his brother physically and a disaster in his heart spiritually. Don't think for a moment that the way you handle your money for God doesn't affect every other area of your life in God. There is a direct correlation.

1 Timothy 6:10 says:

1 Timothy 6:10 [10] For the love of money is the root of all kinds of evil. And some people, craving money, have wandered from the true faith and pierced themselves with many sorrows.

Money is not the root of all kinds of evil, but the love of money is. Not sex. Not power. Not control. Not pride. Money. The love of money is the root of all kinds of evil.

If I don't take what God says about money seriously why would I take seriously what He says about murder, sex, leadership, relationships, or anything else? Jesus Himself placed an incredibly high value on the attitude of money in our hearts. He is recorded in Matthew 6:24 saying:

Matthew 6:24 [24] "No one can serve two masters. For you will hate one and love the other; you will be devoted to one and despise the other. You cannot serve both God and money.

Again, He could have said you cannot serve both God and the devil, or sin, or pleasure, but He didn't. He said, "You cannot serve both God and money." Jesus knew, the number one competitor for our hearts is money, and the stuff it provides (i.e. possessions, prestige, popularity, power).

How we view and handle money in our lives is the greatest test of where our hearts and minds are with God. Our attitude towards money reflects our attitude towards God. It's a spiritual thermometer. Again, in Matthew 6, Jesus is recorded saying:

Matthew 6:21 [21] **Wherever your treasure** (money) **is, there the desires of your heart will also be.**

So, let me ask us a question. If someone who didn't know you were to take ten minutes to look at how you used your money, what would they walk away saying you desired most? Would Jesus or His Church even make the list?

I hope we're all sensing the incredible power our financial decisions have on our spiritual lives. The way we handle money is much more than a financial issue, it is a spiritual one as well. It affects every area of our life.

Remember, honoring God financially is not a burden for us to bear, it's a blessing for us to live. And that's the final principle we have to understand. When the first is given to God the rest is blessed by God.

When I say, "the rest is blessed," I'm not just talking about the money either. This principle is so powerful. I believe, when we honor God financially with the first (tithe), our whole life is blessed in "the rest".

Look at these final words of God to Cain:

Genesis 4:11-12 [11] **Now you are cursed and banished from the ground, which has swallowed your brother's blood.** [12] **No longer will the ground yield good crops for you, no matter how hard you work! From now on you will be a homeless wanderer on the earth."**

I believe this curse goes beyond the murder of Abel and is directly connected to his attitude toward money. Remember, God didn't accept Cain's leftovers, so Cain was angry at God and he let his attitude toward money lead to the murder of his family member.

Because of this, God says the land he would work will be cursed. This sounds an awful lot like what God says in Malachi 3:8-12 concerning the tithe:

Malachi 3:8-12 [8] "Should people cheat God? Yet you have cheated me! "But you ask, 'What do you mean? When did we ever cheat you?' "You have cheated me of the tithes and offerings due to me. [9] You are under a curse, for your whole nation has been cheating me. [10] Bring all the tithes into the storehouse so there will be enough food in my Temple. If you do," says the LORD of Heaven's Armies, "I will open the windows of heaven for you. I will pour out a blessing so great you won't have enough room to take it in! Try it! Put me to the test! [11] Your crops will be abundant, for I will guard them from insects and disease. Your grapes will not fall from the vine before they are ripe," says the LORD of Heaven's Armies. [12] "Then all nations will call you blessed, for your land will be such a delight," says the LORD of Heaven's Armies.

When we choose to not honor God with the tithe, it creates a closed window between us and God. He might want to give us a blessing, but He can't. Or a better way to say it is, He won't. Not because He doesn't want to, but because we haven't opened the window by surrendering the tithe to Him.

God said, **"Try it, put me to the test!"** It's the only place in all the Bible that God says we can test Him. The only place! Do you think God understands how big of an issue this is when the only place we're allowed to test Him is with our money? He's trying to reassure us, "I don't just want something from you, I want something for you."

God never demands something from us because He needs it, He demands something from us because He knows what we need. We need His blessing, provision, and protection, which is only promised through our surrender!

Honoring God financially is not a burden for us to bear, it's a blessing for us to live. So, I will rise-up and honor God financially with every resource He has given me. I will acknowledge that everything I have comes from Him and doesn't belong to me. I'll return to Him the first and best of my income as a sign of my trust in Him, and a way to worship Him. I will not allow my attitude towards money or possessions to negatively affect my relationship with Him, and I will live in the blessing that only He can give.

This is my declaration!

NINE

LIVE FOR ETERNITY

It's only in living for something beyond this life that we'll have anything worth living for in this life.

Have you ever had someone in your life you wanted to be like? Ever have someone you wanted to emulate? For me, from about the age of thirteen to eighteen, I wanted to be like Mike. Not just any Mike though. Some of you already know who I'm talking about, I'm taking about *the* Mike. Michael Jordan.

There used to be an old Gatorade commercial and jingle that became the mantra of my soul. "Like Mike. If I could be like Mike. I wanna be, I wanna be like Mike." [1] But I didn't just want to be like Mike, I wanted to *be* him. I'm pretty sure my 9th grade year of High School I wore a Michael Jordan t-shirt every day to school.

My twin brother Jeremy and I had an old VHS tape (ask your grandparents about VHS or google it) called, *"Michael Jordan: Come fly with me".* [2] It was a video all about the life and career of Michael Jordan. We wore that tape out. Every day before school we watched that video, wanting to be, even believing we could be like Mike.

Our entire lives were built around the belief and expectation that we would one day have songs written about us. We would be on the t-shirts other kids wore. We would have videos made about our lives and careers. Our only plans in life were to not only make it to the NBA, but to dominate it like MJ did.

Jeremy believed this so much that when we were fifteen years old, during an argument with my cousin about our future in basketball, he said, "I'll bet you $1,000 I make it to the NBA." It seemed like a sure bet at the time. This was our pursuit in life. It was our destiny!

To this day, with all of us in our 40's, my cousin will ask for the $1,000 saying, "You need to pay up. You didn't make it to the NBA." My brother always replies, "There's still time man. Until I'm dead, there's still time."

As you can guess, neither of us made it to the NBA. Not even close. My brother is a successful accountant with a beautiful family, living happily in Missouri. I live in Wyoming, leading a Church, loving my family, and laughing at how we used to be, striving toward our far-fetched dreams.

There is nothing wrong with dreams by the way. I think it's good for us to dream. It's dreams that build cities, create cultures, and change policies. It was a dream, captured in one of the most beautiful speeches our world has ever heard, that helped spark and continue changes in our nations racial divide. So again, I have nothing against dreams. I have some even now.

What are your dreams? What do you want to accomplish? What do you live for? That really is the question.

What would have happened if my brother and I did make it to the NBA? If I made it to the NBA, I would have accomplished a childhood dream. I probably would have made tons of money, and possibly experienced fame. If I was good enough I'd have songs made about me and videos highlighting my life, but then what?

If you're lucky, an NBA career might last ten years. Ten years of fame and fortune. Then what? It's sad to me, but there are countless stories out there of athletes, actors, businessmen, (fill in the blank), who achieve their earthly dreams, only to realize it didn't fulfill their eternal soul, and we are no different.

So many times, especially as men, we are living for something else in this life. We pursue pleasure, chase purpose, and crave power. We try to build bigger, better, and bolder things in the search to ease the burning in our hearts for more.

The problem is, none of it works. Nothing in this life will satisfy. It's only in living for something beyond this life that we'll have anything worth living for in this life. We have to rise-up and live for eternity.

When I say, "live for eternity," I'm not just talking about eternal life. I'm talking about living life with eternity in mind. Living life with purpose in every step. In the Bible, Paul understood this concept perfectly.

> IT'S ONLY IN LIVING FOR SOMETHING BEYOND THIS LIFE THAT WE'LL HAVE ANYTHING WORTH LIVING FOR IN THIS LIFE.

Most of us know Paul, but in case you don't, Paul has an incredible story. Based on New Testament history, Paul started fourteen Churches that we know of. He wrote thirteen of the twenty-seven New Testament letters, and almost two-thirds of the book of Acts is following the life, ministry, and impact of the Apostle Paul.

After following Jesus for thirty-two years of his life, the final ones spent in a prison cell for his faith, he would die a martyr's death at the hands of the Roman regime. Outside of Jesus, Paul is perhaps the most significant and influential person in Christian history.

But Paul didn't start off as an Apostle, did he? Paul didn't start off as a messenger for Jesus, he was first a murderer of those who followed Jesus. Literally, Paul started out hating Jesus and hating Christians.

His birth name was Saul and after the resurrection of Jesus, Saul went around arresting and killing men and women who believed in Jesus. His mission was to wipe out Christianity from the face of the earth.

One day, while on his way to arrest more Christians, Jesus appeared to Saul on the road to Damascus. He told him, "I have chosen you to be my messenger to the Gentiles." (Acts 9:15-16) Saul put his faith in Christ, began using his Roman name "Paul," started preaching to both Jews and Gentiles all over the Roman world, and as they say, "the rest is history."

LIVING FOR ETERNITY MEANS I CHOOSE TO LIVE LIKE EVERY MOMENT MATTERS AND EVERY SECOND COUNTS.

It was that same Paul who understood this idea of purpose more than anyone! After his salvation experience and being commissioned by Christ Himself to be a messenger to the world, Paul understood that until he lived for something beyond this life he had nothing worth living for in this life. It was the understanding of his purpose which created a sense of urgency in Paul's life.

In 2 Corinthians 9, Paul says this:

2 Corinthians 9:24-26 [24] Don't you realize that in a race everyone runs, but only one person gets the prize? So run to win! [25] All athletes are disciplined in their training. They do it to win a prize that will fade away, but we do it for an eternal prize. [26] So I run with purpose in every step.

Are we running to win? Are we living with purpose in every step? Are we, like Paul, living for eternity? I believe, in order to be a man and in order to live in Biblical manhood, we need to understand what this means. Living for eternity means I choose to live like every moment matters and every second counts.

Guys, the clock is ticking in our lives. The Bible warns us repeatedly that we are but a breath, a mist, here for a moment and then gone forever. In the Psalms, King David reminds us of this:

Psalm 90:12 - Teach us to realize the brevity of life, so that we may grow in wisdom.

Psalm 39:4- **Lord, remind me how brief my time on earth will be. Remind me that my days are numbered—how fleeting my life is.**

For me, I only have one chance to lead my wife. One opportunity to train my children. One season to minister at Element Church. One window to be a friend. One life to do what I'm called to do, go where I'm called to go, and be who God designed me to be. I only have one chance.

If that's true, I better be living for something beyond this life so that I have something worth living for in this life. Paul understood, he was living for eternity. Every moment mattered, and every second counted, so he was going to run with purpose in every step.

How did he do it? How did he live for eternity, with purpose in every step? Paul finished this life with the next one in mind. I want to do the same! I almost feel like a teenager again, hearing that Gatorade song. Only this time it's not, "Like Mike," it's "Like Paul." "I want to be like Paul!"

There is one conversation Paul had with some trusted friends which I believe captures the principles of his life. Paul reveals for us just how he lived for eternity, and it's the only way we will as well.

In Acts 20, Paul began a journey that would lead to his arrest, a jail cell in Ceaserea, a trial for his faith, and an eventual transfer to Rome where he would die in prison.

Acts 20:18-21 [18] **When they** (his friends) **arrived he declared, "You know that from the day I set foot in the province of Asia until now** [19] **I have done the Lord's work humbly and with many tears. I have endured the trials that came to me from the plots of the Jews.** [20] **I never shrank back from telling you what you needed to hear, either publicly or in your homes.** [21] **I have had one message for Jews and Greeks alike—the necessity of repenting from sin and turning to God, and of having faith in our Lord Jesus.**

In these words, I see that Paul had the heart of God. Now, you might be thinking, "No doubt Paul had the heart of God. He had such courage, faith and boldness," but I'm not talking about that. I agree, he had that, but that's not what I'm talking about.

I'm not even talking about Paul's forgiveness through salvation or the filling of the Spirit in his heart through sanctification. Here is what I'm talking about when I say that Paul had the heart of God. Paul's heart was always concerned for and always focused on the lost.

If we're going to live for eternity. If we're going to live as if every moment matters and every second counts, then we have to become consumed with the things that consume God, and Paul knew first hand, God is consumed with a passion to reach the lost.

In Luke 19:10 Jesus says:

Luke 19:10 - For the Son of Man came to seek and save those who are lost.

Again, in Mark 2:17 Jesus says:

Mark 2:17 - When Jesus heard this, he told them, "Healthy people don't need a doctor—sick people do. I have come to call not those who think they are righteous, but those who know they are sinners."

Even in the most famous verses of all time, John 3:16-17, Jesus reveals to us the heart of God:

John 3:16-17 [16] For God loved the world so much that he gave his one and only Son, so that everyone who believes in him will not perish but have eternal life. [17] God sent his Son into the world not to judge the world, but to save the world through him.

If anyone captured this heart it was Paul. Paul's heart for the lost was unmatched by any human in Scripture, and outpaced only by Christ

Himself, who was God in the flesh. I'm not aware of a clearer example of Paul's heart for the lost than this:

Romans 9:2-3 ²My heart is filled with bitter sorrow and unending grief ³for my people, my Jewish brothers and sisters. I would be willing to be forever cursed—cut off from Christ! — if that would save them.

What? Do you know what Paul is saying? He's saying, "I'd be willing to go to hell if it meant that the Jewish people would put their faith in Christ." If I'm asking for volunteers, none of us are raising our hands for that, including me, right? I'm not there yet. I don't know if I'll ever be there.

NO MATTER WHAT YOU DO FOR A CAREER, YOUR ULTIMATE CALLING IS TO SEE PEOPLE CONVERTED TO CHRIST.

Paul understood what we need to understand. No matter what you do for a career, your ultimate calling is to see people converted to Christ.

Paul was living for something beyond this life, salvation! Not just his salvation, but those who were yet to believe. He knew by living for something beyond this life, it gave him something worth living for in this life. Here's what he wrote in Philippians:

Philippians 1:21-22 - For to me, living means living for Christ, and dying is even better. ²²But if I live, I can do more fruitful work for Christ. So I really don't know which is better.

Paul knew where he was going if he died, which is important, but he also knew what he could do if he lived! Every moment mattered, and every second counted for Paul. If he was going to be alive, he would do everything he could to see more people live in Jesus. If he was going to die, he would be ready to stand face to face with Jesus.

Not only was Paul consumed with the heart of God, but he was careful to listen to the voice of God. In Acts 20, continuing the conversation with his friends, Paul said this:

Acts 20:22-23 [22] **"And now I am bound by the Spirit to go to Jerusalem. I don't know what awaits me,** [23] **except that the Holy Spirit tells me in city after city that jail and suffering lie ahead.**

This wasn't an isolated incident by the way. If you read from Acts chapter 9 through the end of the book, time and time again, Paul not only had the heart of God, but He heard the voice of God and obeyed. Even when it wasn't what Paul would have chosen for himself, he chose to obey the voice of God.

Paul said, "The Holy Spirit tells me…" It's ironic to me that in our American Christianity when someone says, "The Holy Spirit tells me," it's typically never followed by, "jail and suffering lie ahead." But that's what Paul heard, and that's indeed where Paul was headed.

Typically, when Christians say they've heard from God it's for abundance, favor, blessing, and provision. Most times, when we say we heard from God, it's for something good in our life. Something that will make our lives better. Sometimes, we'll even claim we heard God say things about our life that are contrary to the Word He's already given in life.

Listen, God will never tell you to do something that is contrary to His Word. You might have heard someone tell you it was ok, but if it goes against His Word, it wasn't God. But I digress.

I think sometimes we wrongly assume that God's voice will always be for something good in our life. Our definition of good. So, if His voice doesn't fall into my definition of "good," then it must not be from God. This is why I need to have the heart of God, but also be able to hear the voice of God.

We're great at adding caveats to the voice of God, aren't we? "God, whatever it takes for me, my kids, or my spouse to be at the center of Your will…except that!"

Paul had God's heart. His desire was for people to be saved. He was willing to do whatever it took and go wherever he could to reach more people for Jesus. Even jail! Am I on board with going to jail if it means more people will be set free from sin? Paul saw the prison cell as an opportunity to live out his purpose for God.

I want what Paul had because what Paul had we desperately need. I want to have the heart of God and hear the voice of God like Paul did. Lastly, I want the hope of God firmly anchored in my soul. This was evident in the life of Paul.

Here's why having all three of these is so important. If I have the heart of God, but I don't listen to His voice, I won't go very far. The moment I think I hear God say something that does not match my definition of "good," I'm out! If I hear God's voice, but don't have His hope anchored in my soul, I won't last very long. God's voice will often take me through hard times, and without the hope of God I will crumble under the pressure.

Think about the conversation Paul was having with his friends. He said, "My life has been defined by one thing, telling people about the wonderful grace of Christ. Because of that, I don't know what lies ahead. All I know is the Holy Spirit told me, in city after city, that jail and suffering are on its way."

> PAUL SAW THE PRISON CELL AS AN OPPORTUNITY TO LIVE OUT HIS PURPOSE FOR GOD.

Then Paul concludes his words with this:

Acts 20:24 ²⁴ But my life is worth nothing to me unless I use *it* for finishing the work assigned me by the Lord Jesus—the work of telling others the Good News about the wonderful grace of God.

It's only in living for something beyond this life that we'll have anything worth living for in this life. Paul's hope was firmly rooted, not in what would happen to him, but in Who was going with him. He was going with the Lord!

He said, "My life is worth nothing to me, unless!" You see, Paul was not saying that his life was worth nothing. Paul was saying that his life was worth nothing, unless he lived it with the heart of God, heard and obeyed the voice of God, and had his hope rooted in the work of God.

It was this heart, this hearing, and this hope that would eventually lead Paul to a prison cell in Rome. In that cell, Paul would give his life for the faith. Before he died though, Paul wrote several of our New Testament letters and the Gospel message would be launched further than he could have ever imagined, right into the time and space you are reading now.

Paul was living for eternity. Are you? It's only in living for something beyond this life that we'll have anything worth living for in this life. Our jobs are temporary. Our careers are seasonal. Nothing we do in this life really matters, unless it's achieving some sort of impact for the next.

Famous missionary, C.T. Studd (no relation to me by the way) said in a poem, "Only one life 'twill soon be past. Only what's done for Christ will last." [3]

What are you doing for Christ? What "work" has God assigned to you? Paul said his life was worth nothing unless he finished the work God gave him.

God's given you a work to do as well. Each of us are uniquely designed by God to fulfill a God sized purpose for God. It may not be to preach, plant Churches, or die a martyr's death, but it's your task. Are you living it?

You may not know what it is yet, but you can start somewhere. Sign up to serve at your Church. Pray for an opportunity to share your faith at work. Come alongside someone new to the faith and help them follow Jesus. Pick up my previous book, *"Because You're Called: Three Words That Will Change Your Life"*, if you need some help discovering what your calling is.

I don't know what it is for you but start somewhere. Why? Because it's only in living for something beyond this life that we'll have anything worth living for in this life.

So, I will rise-up and seek to have the heart of God, understanding that no matter my career, it's my calling to see more people come to know Christ through me. I will hear the voice of God, going wherever He wants me to go, and doing whatever He wants me to do. I will anchor my faith in the hope of God, living my life as if it's worth nothing to me unless I use it for finishing the work God gave me.

This is my declaration!

TEN

LEAD COURAGEOUSLY

As men, leading courageously is not the absence of fear it is the absence of self.

The story of Desmond Doss captivated me as I watched the portrayal of his life in the 2016 release of the movie called, "*Hacksaw Ridge*".[1] If you don't know, Desmond served in the United States Army during World War II as a combat medic. Twice, he was awarded the Bronze Star, and was also awarded the Medal of Honor for his actions in the Battle of Okinawa.

Lots of people have received the Medal of Honor, but what makes Doss' story so significant is he was the only conscientious objector to receive the Medal during the war. Being raised a devout Seventh-Day Adventist, Desmond was instilled with a strong "non-violence" conviction. So much so that when he joined the army, he refused to even carry or hold a weapon.

His unwavering commitment to his faith and non-violence conviction led to ridicule from his fellow soldiers, even pressure from the Army to send Doss to a conscientious objector camp. Doss, believing the war was justified but refusing to kill another human himself, wanted to serve both God and country as a medic and was eventually allowed to do so.

Joining the 77th Infantry Division, Doss would make his way with the other soldiers to the Battle of Okinawa. Hacksaw Ridge was the nickname soldiers gave to a battlefield that was located on top of a

400-foot cliff, heavily guarded and patrolled by Japanese forces. The control of this battleground was key to winning the war.

In April of 1945, under heavy machine gun and artillery fire, a retreat order was given to the U.S. and Allied troops. While hundreds of soldiers fled down the 400-foot cliff by rope, Doss remained alone at the top, running into the kill zone to carry out wounded soldiers one at a time. As an unarmed medic, he refused to leave any soldier behind, risking his own life to save the lives of others.

One by one, Desmond would support, carry, or drag wounded soldiers to the edge of the cliff and lower them down to safety. Following each life that he saved Doss would pray out loud, "Lord, please help me get one more." After only one night on the battlefield, courageously saving men one at a time, Doss ended up rescuing an estimated 75 soldiers. Some will even say it was closer to 100 soldiers he saved.

If asked, I doubt Doss would have said there was an absence of fear in this courage. The battle of Okinawa was one of the bloodiest in human history. The things those men were required to see, endure, and do is enough to make the bravest of warrior's tremble. The courage of Desmond Doss is not summed up in the absence of fear, I believe it is summed up in the absence of self.

Men, we must rise-up and lead with that same kind of courage. There is a battle we all must face. It's not a battle over political ideologies or military power. It is not waged with guns and ammo. It's a spiritual war we all must face. A battle for our purity and integrity. A battle to take responsibility with our life, leading our family, friends, and loved ones with a bold faith. It's a battle to honor God financially, live for eternity with every breath, and lead courageously.

The things we'll be required to face, the places we're required to go, and the things we'll be required to do might cause a bit of fear and anxiety in us. What God has called us to do as men is no easy task. It will require the strength and resolve that only the Holy Spirit can give. When called to lead like this, I don't believe God is asking us to go without fear. I believe God is asking us to go without self.

As men, leading courageously is not the absence of fear it is the absence of self.

AS MEN, LEADING COURAGEOUSLY IS NOT THE ABSENCE OF FEAR IT IS THE ABSENCE OF SELF.

That's where we've been corrupted as men. Every man wants to be courageous. It's hardwired into our soul. The problem is, we've been relying on the wrong definition of courage our whole lives. We've equated courage with the absence of fear. If that is the definition, then Jesus Himself, who I believe is the most courageous person to ever live, would not fit the description.

On the night that Jesus was arrested, while praying in the Garden of Gethesemene, He was distraught over what lie ahead. The weight that He was carrying and the pain He would have to endure was overwhelming. Both Matthew and Mark's Gospel say that Jesus was, "crushed with grief to the point of death." (Matthew 26:38 and Mark 14:34)

Luke records that Jesus was in such agony of the spirit that as He prayed, His sweat fell like drops of blood. Some scholars believe He actually sweat drops of blood.

Yet in the midst of such agony, anguish, and despair, He didn't face it without fear, He faced it without self. In His prayer, while begging the Father for another way, He poured out these famous words:

Luke 22:42 "Yet, I want Your will to be done not mine!"

His desire for pleasing the Father and His passion for pursuing us was greater than His desire to please Himself.

This is the crux of the issue. It is the core that holds it all together. We can either take what was started in us; the aggression meant to protect, authority meant to inspire, resources meant to provide, purpose meant to change the world, and choose to lead with courage…the absence of self. Or we can take those things, point them inward, and use them to please ourselves.

I believe courage is something that God has already given to us as men. I believe this because in 1 Corinthians 16 it says:

1 Corinthians 16:13-14 [13] **Be on guard. Stand firm in the faith. _Be courageous_. Be strong.** [14] **And do everything with love.** (emphasis added)

The phrase "Be Courageous," comes from the Greek word "andrizó". It's a verb that means, "I act like a man, am brave." [2]

A figurative meaning given from the HELPS Word-Studies is, "To be responsible and courageous by taking the initiatives God reveals through faith."

Hello! We just need God to awaken the courage that's already in us and enable us to lead with it. We need men who will rise-up and lead courageously.

This for me is a life and death matter. I see the potential that waits for us in Christ. I believe this is a game changing, life altering, city revitalizing, and Church revolutionizing opportunity that God wants to awaken in our souls. The enemy would like nothing more than to shut us down. That's why, by the authority and power of Jesus Christ, we need to rise-up, be men, and lead courageously!

So, what does it take to lead courageously? How do we do that? This might surprise you, but I believe in the life of Noah we see some great principles for leading courageously. Yes, there are many courageous men and women in the Bible we could learn from, but something about Noah stood out to me.

Genesis 6:5-8 [5] **The LORD observed the extent of human wickedness on the earth, and he saw that everything they thought or imagined was consistently and totally evil.** [6] **So the LORD was sorry he had ever made them and put them on the earth.**

It broke his heart. [7] And the LORD said, "I will wipe this human race I have created from the face of the earth. Yes, and I will destroy every living thing— all the people, the large animals, the small animals that scurry along the ground, and even the birds of the sky. I am sorry I ever made them." [8] But Noah found favor with the LORD.

RIGHTEOUSNESS FROM GOD IS A NATURAL RESULT OF WALKING IN CLOSE FELLOWSHIP WITH GOD.

Out of all the things which could be written about a man, that has to be one of the best. The last line in verse 8 should be our sole desire and our hearts cry. God looked at the extent of the wickedness on the earth, it broke His heart, but Noah found favor with the Lord.

Genesis 6:9 [9] This is the account of Noah and his family. Noah was a righteous man, the only blameless person living on earth at the time, and he walked in close fellowship with God.

Men, I don't think it was a coincidence that Noah walked in "close fellowship with God" *and* he was a righteous and blameless man. So often we want everything to fall into place spiritually without having to walk in close fellowship with God regularly. Righteousness from God is a natural result of walking in close fellowship with God.

Genesis 6:10-14 [10] Noah was the father of three sons: Shem, Ham, and Japheth. [11] Now God saw that the earth had become corrupt and was filled with violence. [12] God observed all this corruption in the world, for everyone on earth was corrupt. [13] So God said to Noah, "I have decided to destroy all living creatures, for they have filled the earth with violence. Yes, I will wipe them all out along with the earth! "Build a large boat...

Now, from this point God goes on to give Noah the dimensions for the boat he was to build, the type of wood he needed to use, and what to do when it was completed. This boat would be 450-feet long, 75-feet wide, 45-feet high, with a door on one side, and three decks on the inside.

God then told Noah that He would cover the earth with a flood and destroy every living thing. His instructions were to take himself, his wife, his sons (and their wives), and enter the boat. He also said to take on a pair of every kind of animal, both male and female, and enough food to feed his family and all the animals for an extended period of time.

I don't know about you, but if I were Noah I might have stopped God after the word "boat." "You want me to build a boat how big?" I know my current building skills so the thought of building a boat of any size, let alone 450-feet long, would have been enough to handle for one day.

> **GOD WON'T ALWAYS GIVE THE DETAILS OF HOW IT WILL WORK OUT BECAUSE HE'S LOOKING IN US FOR A DESIRE TO OBEY HIM NO MATTER WHAT.**

To put this into perspective, that's twice as long as a Boeing 747, one and a half times the length of a football field, or three space shuttles could lay end to end on the deck of that boat. That's just the length. With its height, width and three decks, if my math is correct, the ark would have been 101,250 square feet of space.

God didn't stop there though. On top of building a boat larger than anything any human had ever seen, He also told Noah to gather a pair of every animal, as well as enough food to feed the animals and his family for a long length of time. Notice though, God never told Noah how to do this or where to find the animals or food.

This is important to note. God won't always give the details of how it will work out because He's looking in us for a desire to obey Him no matter what.

On top of what seems to be insurmountable odds, Noah had to live out his obedience in full view of everyone around him. He had to be thinking, "What will people say? How do I explain this?" Think of all the questions people would ask, and then the other questions they would have after you gave them the answers.

Friends, neighbors, and loved ones would be saying things like: "You're building a boat how big? How will you get it into the water?" "A flood is coming? Why would you think that?" "God told you? What else did he tell you?" "How will you get a pair of every animal into the boat, where will you find all that food, and how will you survive with them in the boat once you're trapped inside?"

I mean, think about it. Would you blame people for having questions? Take off your Sunday School glasses for a moment and think about what God was asking Noah to do. God had literally laid out what was, if we didn't know the rest of the story, an impossible task to complete. Look though, at how Noah responded.

Genesis 6:22 [22] **So Noah did everything exactly as God had commanded him.**

As men, leading with courage is not the absence of fear it is the absence of self, and the first thing Noah did to lead courageously is to risk his reputation. Let me tell you men, if we are going to lead with courage we will have to risk ours as well.

I think the hardest part for Noah in this whole situation was not building the ark, it was having to face what people said and thought about him for building it. The same might be true for us.

When we take drastic measures to rise-up and get aggressive at purity, it is going to stand out. In a world that is filled with pursuing pleasure, if you start pursuing purity you will come under attack.

When we rise-up and take responsibility, living our lives to advance those around us, we'll be accused of having ulterior motives. When we live out our purpose with reckless abandon and honor God first with our finances, people will think we've lost our minds. In other words, in order to lead courageously we will have to risk our reputation as men.

Biblical manhood is not about how we appear to other men, it's about how God appears in me as a man. When we choose to lead courageously, we'll stand out from the crowd. It will potentially separate us from family. We could lose friends, and it might sever even the closest of relationships.

> BIBLICAL MANHOOD IS NOT ABOUT HOW WE APPEAR TO OTHER MEN, IT'S ABOUT HOW GOD APPEARS IN ME AS A MAN.

Until I'd rather risk my reputation with men than lose my relationship with God I'll never lead courageously with my ¯ life. Remember, leading courageously is not the absence of fear, it's the absence of self.

Noah did everything, exactly as God said in spite of what other people thought. This wasn't a one-time thing either. He didn't pick up the hammer one day and enter the boat the next. In order for Noah to lead courageously, he didn't just risk his reputation for a day, he risked it for decades. He had to run with resolution the "race" God had set before him.

Genesis 7:1 [1] **When everything was ready, the LORD said to Noah, "Go into the boat with all your family, for among all the people of the earth, I can see that you alone are righteous."**

As far as we can tell there is approximately 80-120 years of missing information between Genesis 6:22, where Noah did everything as God said, and Genesis 7:1, when everything was ready. Do you know what that tells me? The details of how Noah accomplished the task don't matter as much as the determination he had to finish it. He not only risked his reputation, but he ran with resolution, all the way to the end.

I don't know what plans Noah had before God called him to build the boat, but those plans were now gone. Noah had to set aside his personal preference and preferred future to pursue the purpose of God in his life. Talk about a selfless act. That takes courage!

Like Paul, Noah was saying, "My life is worth nothing to me, unless I use it for finishing the work assigned me by the Lord." (Acts 20:24)

Genesis 7:4-10 [4] Seven days from now I will make the rains pour down on the earth. And it will rain for forty days and forty nights, until I have wiped from the earth all the living things I have created." [5] So Noah did everything as the LORD commanded him. [6] Noah was 600 years old when the flood covered the earth. [7] He went on board the boat to escape the flood—he and his wife and his sons and their wives. [8] With them were all the various kinds of animals—those approved for eating and for sacrifice and those that were not—along with all the birds and the small animals that scurry along the ground. [9] They entered the boat in pairs, male and female, just as God had commanded Noah. [10] After seven days, the waters of the flood came and covered the earth.

> NOAH HAD TO SET ASIDE HIS PERSONAL PREFERENCE AND PREFERRED FUTURE TO PURSUE THE PURPOSE OF GOD IN HIS LIFE.

So many things stand out to me here that we don't have time to discuss. One, the fact that Noah's family stuck with him through all of this is inspiring. While he was most likely losing the respect of everyone else around him, his family not only stuck with him but probably worked for him and then followed him into the boat.

Remember, God didn't speak to Noah's family, He spoke to Noah. Noah could only relay to his wife and kids what God had told him they were supposed to do. Noah led courageously, and his family followed. I hope and pray that I lead in such a way that my wife and children will follow me to do whatever God tells us to do, no matter the cost.

Second, Noah was 600 years old when this happened. That's a six with two zeros. Now, I know the lifespan of people in his day is not fair to compare, but still. This tells me that you're never too old to do what God tells you to do or go where God tells you to go. Leading doesn't end just because our end is drawing near.

The thing that stands out to me most though, and what I want to focus on here, is how Noah seemed to rest in the reliability of God. In order to lead courageously I have to come to grips with the fact that God knows more than me, He wants what's best for me, and He has a plan for me. If He tells me, "This is the way to do it," then I need to do it with no questions asked. You'll never lead courageously without resting in God's reliability.

> YOU'LL NEVER LEAD COURAGEOUSLY WITHOUT RESTING IN GOD'S RELIABILITY.

God said, "Get in the boat and in seven days I'm going to send rain." Maybe you're a way better Christian than me, in fact you probably are, but if God said it would rain in seven days, do you know when I'd want to get in the boat? On the eve of the 7th day.

"Why do we have to get in now, God? It stinks in there, and it's stuffy. The cats are already on board, and why did we have to bring them anyway? I just want to enjoy the last few days of sunshine. I did everything else you asked me. Why do I have to get in now?" That would be me! But not Noah.

> GOD WILL NEVER ASK ME TO DO FOR HIS MISSION WHAT IS ALSO NOT BEST FOR ME IN THE MOMENT.

I don't think Noah was in the boat wondering if it was going to rain. I don't think he was arguing with God or asking Him about it. Do you know what I think Noah was doing? Simply resting in the reliability of God. "If God said it I'll do it and I'm not going to worry about it."

We would probably feel a lot more rested in our own souls if we stopped trying to figure out the reason God asked us to do something and just started trusting in our reliable God.

God will never ask me to do for His mission what is also not best for me in the moment. That doesn't mean He will never allow me to be hurt, it just means He will always protect my heart!

As men, leading courageously is not the absence of fear, it's the absence of self. Noah found favor with God. He was righteous, blameless, and walked in close fellowship with God. And when God called him to build the boat, he had a choice: Lead courageously or leave cowardly. The same choice is ours as well.

So, I will rise-up, follow God, and lead courageously no matter the cost. I will risk my reputation, run with resolution and rest in the reliability of God. I will not let doubt, discouragement, or difficulty stop me from pursing Jesus and leading those He loves. Though none go with me, I still will follow.

This is my declaration!

ELEVEN

LEAVE A LEGACY

We can either build monuments in our own name or we can be on mission for the sake of the Lord's.

Every man wants to leave a legacy. Deep down inside we have an innate desire to leave something behind to be known for. Whether it's a physical monument or a financial inheritance, all of us want to be known for doing something worthwhile in this life. The only problem is the legacies we want to create are more often about our name than they are the Lord's.

What does it take to leave a legacy? Not much really. All of us leave one. The question is, what *kind* of legacy will we leave behind?

As I look at the landscape of the Church today, I am filled with both fear and anticipation for the future. The potential for God's Church is unlimited, but the problems in the Church are as well. So, every generation has a choice: We can either build monuments in our own name or we can be on mission for the sake of the Lord's.

I don't know about you, but when my time on earth is done I hope I've left a legacy that lasts for the Lord. I don't ever want our Churches to become museums full of men only dreaming of what could have been; I want our Churches to become a mighty movement of men (and women) accomplishing what others could only dream of. In our Churches, I hope we leave a legacy of risk takers and history makers.

> WE CAN EITHER
> BUILD MOMENTS IN
> OUR OWN NAME
> OR WE CAN BE ON
> MISSION FOR THE
> SAKE OF THE
> LORD'S.

When we begin to rise-up and finish what was started in us; as we find purpose in the midst of our pain, get bold in our faith, are aggressive at purity, take responsibility for the authority in our lives, honor God financially, live for eternity, and lead courageously, then we will become who God wants us to be and we'll end up leaving a legacy.

That really is the whole key. Becoming who God wants me to be. I'm not capable of changing you as a man and you're not capable of changing me. Yes, we have influence on one another, but ultimately a lasting legacy comes down to our individual decisions.

If I become who God wants me to be and you become who God wants you to be, continue down that road long enough and we've just seen an entire generation become who God wants them to be. Talk about a legacy!

That's the kind of legacy God wants you to leave. God doesn't care about monuments or inheritances as much as He cares about His mission and investment in your soul. He doesn't want people to know your name, He wants people to know His name through you. How do we do that? By becoming the men God wants us to be.

So, what does it take to leave a legacy by becoming the man God wants me to be? What does it take to finish what was started, be bold in my faith, get aggressive at purity, take responsibility, honor God financially, live for eternity, and lead courageously?

There's a great story about legacy in the Old Testament book of 1 Chronicles. Mark Batterson made this story popular in his book called, "*In A Pit With A Lion On A Snowy Day.*" [1] If you haven't read that book I highly recommend it. It's based on the story of Benaiah.

Now I have to admit, until I read Mark's book I hadn't really paid attention to Benaiah's story. Benaiah never made the flannel graph in

Sunday School when I was growing up. He wasn't turned into a Veggie Tales production and wasn't the main character of many sermons in my life --- none that I remember. But woven into the fabric of these few verses about Benaiah are some incredible principles about building our legacy.

1 Chronicles 11:22a [22] **There was also Benaiah son of Jehoiada, a valiant warrior from Kabzeel.**

For many men, what stands out when we read those words? The valiant warrior part, right? I mean, "valiant warrior" describes just about every stereotypical man movie there is. For the most part, when we hear "valiant warrior," we tend to lean in a bit don't we?

That phrase conjures up images, stories, and movies like *Gladiator*: "My name is Maximus Decimus Meridius, commander of the Armies of the North, General of the Felix Legions, loyal servant to the true emperor, Marcus Aurelius. Father to a murdered son, husband to a murdered wife. And I will have my vengeance, in this life or the next." [2]

Braveheart: "Fight and you may die. Run, and you'll live... at least a while. And dying in your beds, many years from now, would you be willin' to trade *all* the days, from this day to that, for one chance, just one chance, to come back here and tell our enemies that they may take our lives, but they'll never take... *our freedoooooom!*" [3]

300: "No retreat, no surrender; that is Spartan law. And by Spartan law we will stand and fight... and die. A new age has begun. An age of freedom, and all will know, that 300 Spartans gave their last breath to defend it!" [4]

Just thinking of scenes or stories like that and I'm ready to pick up a sword and run into battle, aren't you? **"Benaiah son of Jehoiada, a valiant warrior from Kabzeel."**

As I said, we tend to focus on the valiant warrior part, but the key to that whole verse and the first key to leaving a legacy is not the valiant warrior part, it's the "Son of Jehoiada" part.

If you're not careful, you'll miss the whole thing. You might be thinking, "What do you mean? What's the big deal? It's just telling you who his dad was." Yep! That's it! Benaiah would never have been a valiant warrior in his life if he didn't willingly choose a different destiny than he was given from his dad's life. And neither will you.

Leaving a lasting legacy is not about being who my dad was or wasn't, it's about being who God wants me to be today!

> LEAVING A LASTING LEGACY IS NOT ABOUT BEING WHO MY DAD WAS OR WASN'T, IT'S ABOUT BEING WHO GOD WANTS ME TO BE TODAY!

You see, Jehoida was a Jewish priest. In the Bible, the book of Exodus tells us that only the tribe of Levi, specifically the descendants of Aaron, were set apart from the twelve tribes of Israel to be priests for the Lord. Only the priests were allowed to approach the Lord in the Temple. They were the ones who administered the sacrifices and sacraments, made the offerings, led the worship, spoke to the Lord for the people, and spoke to the people for the Lord.

This means that from the day Benaiah was born he "knew" what he was going to be. He was going to be a priest. Being a priest would have been one of the highest honors among all the men of Israel. There would have been no greater calling for Benaiah than that of a priest, except for one thing. God didn't call Benaiah to be a priest. God called Benaiah to be a valiant warrior.

Guys, the highest honors among men don't make up for missing the heart of the Lord. No matter what is expected of you and no matter what has been passed down to you, only you have the ability to choose to do what God wants for you.

No matter what your dad did or didn't do, and no matter who you have or haven't been, only you can choose to rise-up and become who God wants you to be. Don't let your obligations in the world or your expectations from men keep you from God's opportunity in your life. It's time to rise-up and choose your own destiny!

Yes, our fathers, or lack thereof, play a massive role in who we become as men. But while they may have a part in developing our character only we can choose our destiny in Christ.

How did Jehoida respond when Benaiah told him he wouldn't be a priest? Well, the Bible doesn't tell us, so we don't know. I don't know how Jehoida responded, but I'd like to believe he gave his full support.

Maybe Jehoida was a legacy maker in his own generation. Maybe he was one of the first priests who rose-up and said, "Even though my son is expected to be a priest in this life I am in full support of him living out God's unique purpose for his life."

Whether Jehoida started that legacy or not I don't know, but I do know that Benaiah continued it. Not only did Benaiah choose his own destiny in the Lord, but he apparently led his sons to do the same.

Did you know that Benaiah had two sons who both chose their own destiny as well? One son, Jehoiada, named after his grandfather, became King David's chief counselor. Another son, Ammizabad, became a warrior himself.

As Benaiah's sons grew up I imagine him telling them, "I don't care what is expected of you, I just want you doing what God tells you to do." We should be doing the same. Whether you have children or not, the way we lead the next generation must be a legacy leaving kind of leadership.

WHEN WE CHOOSE OUR DESTINY IN CHRIST WE CAN BE SURE THERE WILL BE ENEMIES AGAINST US BECAUSE OF CHRIST.

We need to say to our sons and daughters, our young men and women, "I don't care what is expected of you I just want you doing what God tells you to do. No matter where it takes you or how much it costs you I will support you to the very end." That's how we leave a lasting legacy. Choose your own destiny, the one *God* has prepared for you!

Choosing our destiny though is only the beginning of leaving a legacy. It's one thing to choose your destiny, it's another thing altogether to chase the enemies that will try and stop you. When we choose our destiny in Christ we can be sure there will be enemies against us because of Christ.

1 Chronicles 11:22b Another time, on a snowy day, he chased a lion down into a pit and killed it.

That's intense, right? I don't know about you, but I want to have that kind of aggression and conviction against the sin in my life and against the enemy of my life.

We've talked about this already in the book, but I want to expound upon it again here. We can't just suppress sin in our lives, it needs to be subdued, destroyed, and defeated.

Genesis 4:7 [7] You will be accepted if you do what is right. But if you refuse to do what is right, then watch out! Sin is crouching at the door, eager to control you. But you must subdue it and be its master.

We must destroy sin in our lives because the devil will not hesitate to defeat our lives with sin.

It wasn't good enough for Benaiah to get the lion in the pit and just suppress it for a while. Benaiah was going in after it and only one of them was coming out alive. Men, if we are going to rise-up and leave a legacy, we've got to be willing to chase our enemies into the pit and not be satisfied until only we walk out alive.

We can't do this on our own. This isn't some sort of egotistical man thing. This is only done through the power of Christ in and through us. If we try to chase the enemy on our own we'll be devoured, but if we choose to chase the enemy with Christ, we know we've already won.

What lions do you need to chase today? What enemies have been weighing you down? I don't know what enemies you're facing today; all I know is, it's time to chase them down. Legacy creators are always lion chasers.

The last thing I see in Benaiah might be the most important thing of all. Once you choose your destiny in Christ and start chasing your enemy with Christ you're going to have to change your weapons because of Christ!

1 Chronicles 11:23 [23] **Once, armed only with a club, he killed an Egyptian warrior who was 7½ feet tall and whose spear was as thick as a weaver's beam. Benaiah wrenched the spear from the Egyptian's hand and killed him with it.**

LEGACY CREATORS ARE ALWAYS LION CHASERS.

There is one detail here that is so important to the legacy making process. Benaiah, with only a club, faced a 7 ½ foot Egyptian warrior whose spear was as thick as a weaver's beam. Why is this important? Well, a weaver's beam would have been 2.5 to 3 inches in diameter. Think about that.

That's the same size or larger than the barrel end of a baseball bat. The spear head for that size of spear would have been around 15 pounds as well. Go find a baseball bat, hold it on the fat end and think about how huge and heavy this weapon would have been.

When Benaiah faced this warrior do you think he felt ready for the fight? His enemy had a spear as thick as a baseball bat with a 15-pound sharpened head on the end of it. What did Benaiah have? A club. But not just "a" club. The Scripture tells us he was armed with "only" a club. This is so huge. Do you know what this tells me?

Benaiah was willing to chase the enemy with what he already had in his hand.

What we are required to face in this life is daunting. I'm not discounting that. The amount of effort and commitment it will take for us to rise-up and be the men God is calling us to be can be an overwhelming thought. So many times, we can look at the legacy we want to leave and the enemies we'll have to face and be overwhelmed by our own lack of ability.

BENAIAH WAS WILLING TO CHASE THE ENEMY WITH WHAT HE ALREADY HAD IN HIS HAND.

We say things like, "I'm not ready. I'm not strong enough. I don't have the right weapons. I don't know enough. The enemy is too strong!" Or whatever it is! Do you know what that sounds like?

Proverbs 22:13 [13] **The lazy person claims, "There's a lion out there! If I go outside, I might be killed!"**

Yes, there are lions outside. They are everywhere, and they will never go away. The reality is, we will never feel like we have enough, know enough, or are capable enough for this fight. That's kind of the point.

It's only when we come to the end of ourselves that Jesus can give us all of Himself. If we only choose our destiny or chase our enemy when we feel like we're ready, we'll never do it. We can't wait for the weapons we want to have, we've got to start moving with the weapons we already have.

That's what God told Gideon when he was questioning his fight against the enemy. God chose Gideon, a man from the weakest clan and smallest tribe in Israel, to lead the nation of Israel in a fight against their enemy.

The army of Midian had overtaken Israel. God calls Gideon to lead an attack against them and Gideon questions the call. He basically asks what all of us ask at some point, "God, how am *I* going to do this?" Look at what God says:

Judges 6:14 [14] **Then the Lord turned to him and said, "Go with the strength you have, and rescue Israel from the Midianites. I am sending you!"**

God told Gideon to go to war with what he had. "Go with the strength you have." Remember, Benaiah went to war with what was already in his hand. So, let me ask you, what weapons do you already have?

I know its cliché, but what about the Word of God? Listen, you will never know the will of God, walk in the way of God, or win the war for God unless you're consistently in the Word of God.

Psalm 119:9 ⁹ **How can a young person stay pure? By obeying your word.**

IT'S ONLY WHEN WE COME TO THE END OF OURSELVES THAT JESUS CAN GIVE US ALL OF HIMSELF.

Hebrews 4:12 ¹² **For the word of God is alive and powerful. It is sharper than the sharpest two-edged sword, cutting between soul and spirit, between joint and marrow. It exposes our innermost thoughts and desires.**

When the Apostle Paul was challenging us to put on every piece of God's armor so that we would be able to resist the enemy and be strong in battle, he said:

Ephesians 6:17 ¹⁷ **Put on salvation as your helmet, and take the sword of the Spirit, which is the word of God.**

Over and over again we are reminded of the power of the Word of God in our lives. Yet there seem to be so many men who are desperate to win the war but not committed to be in the Word. We've got to change our weapons men. We will never win the war by waging battle as the world does.

2 Corinthians 10:3-4 ³ **We are human, but we don't wage war as humans do.** ⁴ **We use God's mighty weapons, not worldly weapons, to knock down the strongholds of human reasoning and to destroy false arguments.**

Men, I believe that everything we need to become everything God wants us to be is already at our disposal. It's already in our hands. There is no magic formula. We just need to change weapons. We need to go with what we already have instead of waiting for what will never come.

When we pair these three things together; when we choose our destiny in Christ, chase our enemy with Christ and change our weapons because of Christ we'll end up leaving a lasting legacy for Christ.

Look at these final words about Benaiah:

1 Chronicles 11:24-25 [24] **Deeds like these made Benaiah as famous as the three mightiest warriors.** [25] **He was more honored than the other members of the Thirty, though he was not one of the Three. And David made him captain of his bodyguard.**

We like the word "famous" don't we? That's what we often think of when we think of leaving a legacy. Yes, Benaiah became famous, but that wasn't his legacy. Benaiah wasn't trying to be famous, like every other Bible story hero, he was simply trying to be faithful to the Famous One (God). Now that's a legacy worth leaving!

Benaiah, son of Jehoida was a valiant warrior. That was his legacy. What's yours? We can either build monuments in our own name or we can be on mission for the sake of the Lord's.

Because I want to leave a lasting legacy with my life I will rise-up and choose my destiny in Christ, chase the enemy with Christ, and change my weapons because of Christ. From this day forward, my name is Jeff, son of Gary, child of God, and I will be a valiant warrior for Jesus!

This is my declaration!

TWELVE

WHO'S YOUR HUSHAI?

I firmly believe that our level of intimacy with men will determine our level of victory as men.

That just freaked some guys out didn't it? Intimacy with men? Just the word intimacy scares most of us, and when we use it in conjunction with another man, well that's just weird.

For most of us hear the word "intimacy," and we immediately think "sexuality." But intimacy is so much more than sexuality. Sex can be a part of intimacy, a necessary part for those who are married, but it is not a required part of intimacy. Last I checked human beings can live without sex, but I'm not sure we can live without intimacy. At least not in a healthy way.

Intimacy means = close familiarity or friendship; closeness.[1]

Intimacy is very difficult for most men, even for those of us who are married. We typically have no problem with the sexual part of intimacy, but we really struggle with the relational part.

To be intimate with someone relationally is to let them see all of who you are on the inside. Someone once described intimacy as, "into-me-see". For a lot of us, we'd rather bare our bodies to someone we don't know than bare our soul to someone we do.

This is why so many men struggle to find victory. We don't allow someone in our life that we can truly tell anything to and who we are willing to tell everything to. But we need that. As I started out saying,

I firmly believe that our level of intimacy with men will determine our level of victory as men.

As men, we shouldn't tell everything about ourselves to everyone, but we should tell everything about ourselves to someone. That's what a Hushai (pronounced "Who-Shy") is and that's what every man needs. So, who's your Hushai? I would tell you about mine first, but I should probably explain where the name comes from.

I love how the most random verses in the Bible can make the greatest impact on your life. Sometimes the most insignificant entries in the Word of God can have the greatest inspiration on the way I live. This is part of why I believe that nothing is in the Bible by accident. Even the lists and genealogies can offer the most heart changing truths to build our lives on. A Hushai is one of those things.

> I FIRMLY BELIEVE THAT OUR LEVEL OF INTIMACY WITH MEN WILL DETERMINE OUR LEVEL OF VICTORY AS MEN.

If you're familiar with the Bible, especially the Old Testament, you know there are lots of lists and names. From genealogies to geography there are just lots of lists in the Bible.

To be honest, sometimes I skim over the lists to get to the "good" stuff. I know that's not what a pastor should say but it's the truth. There are just some days where you can't take any more "begetting". Don't get me wrong, I love a good begetting of my own, but reading about all of it just gets old.

One day, I was flying through the final few chapters of 1 Chronicles for my devotions. I was in 1 Chronicles 27, which is basically one giant list. It lists out all the military commanders in Israel under the authority of King David, the divisions each of those commanders led, and how many were in each division. Then it lists the leaders of each tribe in Israel. (See, your eyes are already rolling back in your head and I'm not even giving you the whole list.)

The chapter continues with a list of all the officials in David's Kingdom. It literally gave the name of the person that was in charge of the king's sheep and goats, and the name of the person in charge of the donkeys. Then, in the final verses of the chapter, it appears to list the people that were closest to King David. Call it his "inner court."

1 Chronicles 27:32-34 ³² **Jonathan, David's uncle, was a wise counselor to the king, a man of great insight, and a scribe. Jehiel the Hacmonite was responsible for teaching the king's sons.** ³³ **Ahithophel was the royal adviser. Hushai the Arkite was the *king's friend*.** ³⁴ **Ahithophel was succeeded by Jehoiada son of Benaiah and by Abiathar. Joab was commander of the king's army.**

Did you see it? **"Hushai the Arkite was the king's friend."** How powerful is that? If you're not careful, you could read right past that and not catch the significance of it.

Here we have an entire chapter of God's Holy Scripture dedicated to listing out the commanders of the army, the tribal leaders, the King's entire work force, his inner circle, and right there among the list is Hushai, the king's friend.

The day this struck me it changed me forever. Even David, mighty warrior, man after God's own heart, leader of the people of Israel, commander of God's army, needed a friend. David needed someone in his personal circle that wasn't affected by the monthly pay cycle. (I'm not sure they got paid monthly, it's just a figure of speech.)

That's what a Hushai is. A Hushai is someone you can tell anything to and it won't affect your position, your pay, their position or their pay, or their perception of you. (Position, pay, perception) In other words, for a Hushai to be a Hushai, they can't work for you and you can't work for them. They can't be your spouse. They probably shouldn't be family, although they might feel more like family than anyone else.

To Hushai, David was not only his king, he was his friend. To David, Hushai wasn't on the payroll, he was a personal confidant. Do you have that? Do you have someone that you can truly tell anything to and it won't affect your position, your pay, or their perception of you? Do you have a person that is truly for you and not what you do? Do you have someone that you could tell anything to, and it wouldn't derail their support of you?

I'm not sure I'd ever had that in my life until I found mine. I'm already an introverted person so friendships don't come easy. I would say I've typically been a person who has lots of acquaintances but not many "close" friends. The few close friends I've had I still kept up a pretty good guard around certain areas of my life.

Being a pastor, this has even been more difficult. I understand the power of the position I've been given. I think most pastors struggle with this as well. It's hard to know who to trust in the Church. In fact, I would even suggest that if you are a pastor, your Hushai should not be in your Church. The problem is, I'm currently breaking that rule myself.

It's hard to tell someone everything about yourself. That's a compromising place to be. Will they still like me? Will they look up to me? Will they even love me if I tell them this? But it's only in this place of vulnerability that we open ourselves up to our greatest victory.

Sin grows in secret. The longer we keep something to ourselves the faster it will lead to sin. In secret, our desires will quickly lead to temptation, jump to sin, and end in death before we know it (James 1:14-15). When kept in the dark, burdens turn into depression, anger into hate, hurts into bitterness, worry into anxiety, and the list goes on. I need someone in my life I can go to with these things.

I need someone in my life I can talk to about my past without worrying about their perception. There are things about me that no one else knows except my wife and my Hushai. There are things about me that *only* my Hushai knows.

I know some people will struggle with me saying this, but there are some things I don't want my wife to carry with me. I'm not saying that we should hide things from our spouse, but I do believe there are some things that we should not place upon them. Some burdens are not for her to carry, but my Hushai can.

I was 40 years old before I found my Hushai. Some of that has to do with me. As I said, I'm a pretty guarded person. In fact, I didn't even go looking for a Hushai. In July of 2015, God brought one to me.

One year prior to finding mine, the closest person I'd ever had to a Hushai moved to a new town. Our Church had just gone through one of the most tumultuous seasons of ministry we'd ever seen. We closed down a campus, had three staff members resign, and the vision we were pursuing as a Church was turned upside down. I was nearly ready to call it quits. Not because I didn't want to be the pastor but because I honestly didn't know if I was the right person for the job.

I knew I needed a "friend," so I had recently started praying for God to bring one into my life. If I'm honest, I was kinda hoping He wouldn't answer. I'm pretty content with my guarded, introverted self, so the thought of bringing someone in who wasn't already there seemed daunting to say the least. But in my heart, I knew I needed someone to trust. I hadn't learned about "Hushai" in the Scripture yet, but Hushai is what I needed.

In a series of events that can only be described as providential, God placed a man in my life named Todd. I had known him for a while as a part of our Church, but only through his wife Kim and her friendship with my wife. So, Todd and I were acquaintances but not much more than that.

During one of our annual outreach events at Element I signed up to serve on a team led by Todd. He then joined us on an exploratory trip to another Wyoming community where we met with someone interested in starting a campus of Element Church. We had coffee a few times, and it finally just clicked.

Todd really is the one who crossed the line first. I jokingly call this our "going out email," because that's what it reminded me of. "Will you go out with me, circle yes or no!"

I'm giving you a window now into my life that makes me uncomfortable, but my prayer is that it will unleash in some men a desire to pursue the unthinkable – an intimate relationship with another man! A Hushai!

My biggest fear in sharing this is that somehow it will reflect poorly upon Todd. Just as Todd is my Hushai, I have become his. I want to be an armor bearer for him, protecting him and his heart at all costs. He's agreed to let me share this, both of us believing it may help someone else find a Hushai in their own life.

On July 24th of 2015, I received the following email and began a conversation with Todd. Some details I've taken out for confidentiality. Just so you know, Todd is an introvert as well:

> July 24th, 2015 at 10:07 AM Todd wrote:
> I'm emailing you because I don't want to interrupt your travels. This way you can respond if and when appropriate. Introverts unite! Lol
>
> I guess by the time I have everything figured out I'll be welcomed into heaven.
>
> I never want to dump my shortcomings on you. I make it a point to not say certain things to you, as a sense of protection to you. You carry such a heavy burden of our community with you constantly. And I will not be a friend that takes advantage of your title. I care about you too much for that. I do feel called to a friendship with you. I think God is telling me that you need a friend who doesn't focus on your title but respects it. It's just a connection I feel - (yoked). Hopefully that doesn't sound too creepy (lol). Maybe you don't feel the same way I do - that's ok.

I've said it before, I don't want our relationship based on Biblical academics but Biblical principles. I mean it when I say this - you can tell me or rebuke me on anything! You can literally say – "Todd, you're an idiot", and it would not affect the care or respect I have for you. I would only say that to men who follow Jesus. Their words have more weight to it.

You should also know, several years ago my wife and I prayed for like-minded friends that we could feel like were family with. I am confident that you and Sabrina are part of that answered prayer. I am so thankful you guys are in our lives. It's my hope that Kim and I can be that way for others.

Thank you for your patience with me and my growth. I guess that's part of letting go of pride and accepting humility, resting in Jesus, while those you love can help you and encourage you through trials.

Thanks for everything. You're a good man, and I'm honored to even be considered to be in your company.

Your friend, Todd.

Keep in mind, Todd had no idea that I had been praying for a friend. He had no idea that I needed someone in my life to do exactly what he felt God was calling him to do. Up until this point, our friendship had been surface level only. He had told me some struggles, but I hadn't really shared any of mine.

Again, I'm guarded, cautious, and leery of doing those things. But I needed it. I desperately needed it in my life. At any other point in my life this email would have sounded weird, but in this moment, it was just right. Here is my response:

July 24th, 2015 at 4:23 PM, Jeff wrote:
You're an idiot! HA HA!

Thanks for sharing that Todd. You gotta be careful what you pray for. God will often answer it. That's why I try not to pray to be humbled, but that God would give me humility! lol

Funny you should talk about being "called" to friendship. I'm a super guarded guy. I let very few people in. I have few friends, and even fewer close friends. With that said, (totally sounds like we are asking each other out, LOL) I have definitely felt a need to have a dude in my life I can hang out with, talk to, be real with and not have the "pastor" hat on.

Being a pastor is who I am so it's impossible to separate it totally, but I have said on more than one occasion to Sabrina how much I love hanging out with you and Kim and can see you as a friend in my life. I appreciate you wanting to be just that. Lots of people want access into our lives BECAUSE we are the pastors. It's hard to find someone who just wants to be friends with Jeff and Sabrina. We feel like you and Kim are that.

I feel like I need to put, "If you want to be my friend, circle yes or no" on our emails. HA HA!

Like I said. I'm super guarded. It's hard for me to open up to friends or even family, so, as long as you're ok putting up with my introverted guarded awkwardness I'm good too! It's so weird that you felt God telling you I needed a friend not concerned with my title. You heard right for sure! That is exactly what I need.

Thanks for being a good friend Todd. I appreciate that more than you know. Also, don't ever hesitate throwing up on me. I don't view that as a "pastoral" thing but a "friend" thing. I wouldn't have let you in this far into my life if I

wasn't comfortable with a little vomit now and then. Thanks for all you do.
Jeff

As I'm writing this chapter, we are coming up on three years of "friendship". To be honest, it feels like we've been friends for 30 years. The level of trust, love, support, and intimacy that has brought in our lives can only be described as a "God thing". I don't know what kind of relationship David and Jonathan had, but we've often talked about how we could see their friendship like our own.

1 Samuel 18:3 ³ **And Jonathan made a solemn pact with David, because he loved him as he loved himself.**

David and Jonathan's friendship has been described as intimate. How would God describe yours with your friends? Do you have that yet? What's stopping you from it? Is it time to start praying for that in your life?

THE BIBLE DOESN'T SAY, BUT I HAVE TO WONDER IF THE GREAT MEN OF THE BIBLE DIDN'T ALSO HAVE GREAT INTIMACY WITH ANOTHER MAN.

This isn't just a David and Jonathan thing either, and it's definitely not a Jeff and Todd thing. I think you see this all throughout the Scriptures. I think you even see this in Jesus Himself. Was John Jesus' Hushai while He walked the earth? Was Silas or Timothy Paul's? Was Joshua a Hushai for Moses, or Caleb a Hushai for Joshua? Did Daniel lean on Shadrach, Meshach and Abednego and did they lean on each other for strength? Did Jeremiah have a Hushai in Baruch?

The Bible doesn't say, but I have to wonder if the great men of the Bible didn't also have great intimacy with another man.

See, even that word is still giving some of you fits. I'm telling you, your level of intimacy with men will determine your level of victory as a man. If you want to finish what was started in you by finding purpose in your pain, being bold in your faith, getting aggressive at purity, taking responsibility, honoring God financially, leading courageously, living for eternity and leaving a legacy, you're not going to do it alone. You're going to need a Hushai, or even a whole group of them.

I can't imagine my life without Todd. I've told him on so many occasions, "Everyone needs a Todd." So far, he has remained true to his word in that initial email. He's just been my friend. I have many great friendships in our Church and on our staff. I could make a list just like David had in 1 Chronicles 27, but right there in the midst of my list would be, "And Todd, Pastor Jeff's friend."

Our relationship was locked, clamped, sealed, and bound into my heart on Sunday, April 17th of 2016. This was a special day at Element because it was baptism Sunday. But this baptism was special to me because on this day, I would be baptizing Todd.

Baptism Sunday's are always moving for me. To see each life that God has impacted through our Church just blows me away. In every baptism service God reminds me, "This is why I called you to Cheyenne." Not that God couldn't have used someone else to start Element, but I think it's a way that God confirms His calling in me. Every baptism story is a confirmation of God's call on my life.

I knew it would be an emotional day. Todd's an emotional guy. Neither he nor I are afraid to shed a few tears now and then, especially when it comes to our family and faith. Up to that point, God had done an incredible work on Todd's heart. In just a few short years at Element Todd had gone from a "check the box" Christian to a called out one. So many parts of his life and faith had been surrendered to God and he had seen the massive transformation that only the Holy Spirit could provide. This baptism was a milestone moment for him.

Not only was I baptizing him, but I also got to baptize his middle daughter, Emma, just before him. Needless to say, his face was wet before he even got in the tank. The tears were already flowing on me as well. I was so proud of my friend. I was so honored to be his

Hushai in that moment. Yes, I was baptizing him as his pastor, but even more so I was celebrating with him as his friend.

I asked him what we ask every baptism candidate, "Do you believe in Jesus as Lord and Savior of your life?" He said it so loud and proud, "EVERY DAY!" As he came up out of the water He raised his arms in the air, fists held high in praise. We were both a blubbering and broken mess. Broken, not in a bad way, but in a great way for the Lord.

As we continued with worship in the service I was again moved to tears. While we were singing I burst out into thanksgiving to God. I thought the same thing about Todd as I thought about every person getting baptized, "God, you brought us here for them." I literally said to God, "God, You brought us here for that moment. You brought us here for Todd."

As if that weren't enough, God spoke back to my heart these words: "Jeff, I didn't just bring you here for Todd, I also brought you here because *you needed Todd.*" I lost it. I almost couldn't compose myself. I didn't know if I'd regain enough composure to preach. Thankfully I did, but I will never be the same again. God didn't just bring me to Cheyenne to help reach Todd, God brought me to Cheyenne so Todd could help reach me.

I can honestly say that I am a stronger husband, father, pastor, friend, son of God, and man because of Todd in my life. God has given us a connection that only He could provide. Yes, I believe our relationship grew faster than normal as the Holy Spirit moved it along, but I know there are victories in my life that would not have happened without my intimacy with Todd.

So, who's your Hushai? Do you have one? Will you allow one? It might start by just getting connected into a men's group. Maybe you need to send out an email like Todd did to me. Perhaps you just need to ask that person who's been on your heart if they'd like to start meeting regularly for coffee. You may not find your Hushai tomorrow, but you need to start looking and praying for one today.

As Todd and I both pursue what it means to be a man, we will do so together through our intimacy as men. Why? Because I firmly believe, our level of intimacy with men, will determine our level of victory as men.

I love you Todd!

This is my declaration!

The following declaration can be downloaded for free at www.jeffmaness.com. There is a specific & unique declaration available for both genders, single or married, with or without kids. The declaration included in this book is the full declaration for married men with kids.

For every person who wants to rise-up and make this their declaration I'm challenging you to download the document, print it, sign it, and proudly display it somewhere in your home.

Maybe you can display it by the front door of your house, or in the living room where your family gathers. Maybe you put it on the bathroom mirror to remind you every day before you leave for work, or perhaps you put it by your desk at work. I don't care where you display the declaration, my biggest prayer is that you'll live it.

Men, let's rise-up and make this "My Declaration!"

If you have yet to put your faith in Jesus as the Savior of your life, that is the first declaration you need to make. Make no mistake about it, Jesus has made a declaration with His life on your behalf.

All of us have sinned. That sin separates us from a holy God. Nothing we can do can bridge the gap between us and God. No amount of work, sum of money, or list of good deeds can earn my salvation.

So, because God loved you so much, He sent Jesus to bridge that gap. Jesus, God in the flesh; He came as one of us, modeled life for us, died because of us, rose victorious, so that any one of us could put our faith in Him, be forgiven of our sins, given a new life today and eternal life forever in Heaven with Him. That is the Good News!

Receiving Christ as your Savior is not a get out of hell free card, it is a live life to the fullest today card! Jesus not only wants to forgive you of your sins, and He will, but He also wants to fill you with the power of the Holy Spirit to live for Him.

If you want to start your life in Jesus today, you can do that by praying this prayer to God. This prayer doesn't save you, Jesus does that, but you get access to Jesus through prayer:

"Father in Heaven, I believe in Jesus. I believe He is the only way to Heaven and the only plan for salvation. So today I give You me! Forgive me of my sins. Wash me clean and make me new. Everything I've ever done against You I confess to You. I repent of the way I have lived. I will turn from my life of sin and follow You in my freedom. I receive from You, salvation. Come live in my heart. Thank you for loving me, Jesus. Please help me to love You back with my whole life. Today, I belong to You. This is my declaration! In Jesus name, Amen."

If you sincerely prayed that prayer to God, CONGRATULATIONS, you are a Christian! That means you have accepted Jesus into your heart and that you are committed to following Him the rest of your life. There is not a more important decision you could ever make. You have now started on an incredible journey of following and loving Jesus.

Next, you should tell someone about your decision to believe in Jesus. Talk to a trusted Christian friend, small group leader, or a pastor. We would love to hear about your decision, so you could even email us at hello@jeffmaness.com.

We are excited for your decision to follow Christ. It is the best decision you will ever make. Welcome to the family of God!

Something was started within us as men, something when we were born. Something was placed there by God Himself that lies dormant and ready to rise. So, no more will we sit idly by while the devil wreaks havoc in our lives. No more will we let down our guard and bask in the comfort of "just good enough". For us, it is time to rise-up!

I will rise-up to finish what God started in me. I will hear what God says about me, do what He tells me to do, and give credit where credit is due. He's not done working in me, nor is He done working through me, so I will simply focus on the next thing He's asking of me.

I will rise-up and live out a bold faith by knowing Who I'm standing in, when I'll stand firm, and why I'm standing strong. I will stand in the Lord, draw an uncompromising line in the sand, and do it all for the glory, honor, and praise of my God.

I will rise-up and use the aggression God gave me toward the purity He expects from me. I will realize what I'm after most, seeking to please Jesus instead of bringing pleasure to myself. I will refuse to even get close, running from all sexual sin. I will resolve to do whatever it takes, taking drastic measures in my Game-Plan for purity.

I will rise-up and take responsibility for the authority God has given me. I will acknowledge where I am, admit who I am, and accept all the blame for what I've done. I will use my authority to promote God at any cost, for the sake of all those He has placed in my life.

I will rise-up and take responsibility for the authority God has given me in my marriage. I will make Jesus my first pursuit, and submission my first priority. I will seek, serve, and spoil my wife, leading her with the same love that Jesus has shown me.

I will rise-up and take responsibility as a father, offering my best to the children God has entrusted me with. I will seek God's counsel for them, surrender my control of them, and stand on God's commitment to them.

I will rise-up and honor God financially with every resource He has given me. I will acknowledge that everything I have comes from Him, give the first and best of my income as a sign of my trust in Him, and not allow money or possessions to negatively affect my relationship with Him so I can live in the blessing that only He can give.

I will rise-up and live for eternity, knowing that every moment matters and every second counts. I will seek to have the heart of God, hear and obey the voice of God, and anchor my faith in the hope of God. I will live my life as if it's worth nothing to me, unless I use it for finishing the work God gave me.

I will rise-up and lead courageously no matter the cost. I will risk my reputation, run with resolution, and rest in the reliability of God. I will not let doubt, discouragement or difficulty stop me from pursing Jesus and leading those He loves. Though none go with me I still will follow.

I will rise-up and leave a lasting legacy. I will choose my destiny in Christ, chase the enemy with Christ, and change my weapons because of Christ. From this day forward, my name is _____, son of _____, child of God, and I will be a valiant warrior for Jesus!

This is My Declaration!

Signed: _____

Date: _____

APPENDIX 1

THE SCIENCE BEHIND SEXUAL SIN

Well, if you found yourself here you are either OCD like me and can't mark that you read a book unless you read the whole book, or you took up my offer from chapter four to consider the issue of purity a little deeper.

Many people believe that Scripture and science are mutually exclusive, but what I hope we'll see here is that Scripture and science can be mutually expressive. Scripture and science go hand in hand, not fist to fist.

Personally, as a follower of Jesus and a pastor in the Church, I think we are too often afraid of science. Somehow, we think that science is our enemy, when it's actually our friend. Just so we're clear, when I say science, I'm talking about more than just physical science. In this Appendix we'll see how physical, psychological and sociological science stands hand in hand and side by side with Scripture.

I can't address every aspect of sexuality here, nor look at all the information available. I'm intentionally leaving out the LGBTQ conversation from this appendix. It is not because I don't think it needs addressed, I just don't believe I can address it with the measure it deserves in this setting. It is far too deep and far too personal for this discussion. I would again point you to the resources I suggested in chapter four.

So, let's look at the four most common questions or pushbacks I get from people concerning sexual purity. I'll start with what many people believe to be the most "innocent" forms of sin, and then move on from there.

1. What's the big deal with pornography?

Pornography statistics are alarming to say the least. With one internet search, you can find hours of reading on the amount of pornography being produced and consumed in America alone. I don't think anyone needs information on the fact that porn, more than ever, is being consumed at massive rates. Nearly all of us carry instant access to graphic porn in our pockets on our phones.

As short as ten years ago sharing statistics about porn would rattle the room, but that has all changed. Now it's common knowledge. What we *are* discovering are the effects of porn, and it's even scarier than the statistics. When people say, "Porn doesn't hurt anyone," they don't understand the half of it.

> Teenagers with frequent exposure to sexual content on TV have a substantially greater likelihood of teenage pregnancy; and the likelihood of teen pregnancy was twice as high when the quantity of sexual content exposure within the viewing episodes was high.
>
> Pornography viewing by teens disorients them during the developmental phase when they have to learn how to handle their sexuality and when they are most vulnerable to uncertainty about their sexual beliefs and moral value.
>
> A significant relationship also exists among teens between frequent pornography use and feelings of loneliness, including major depression.
>
> Adolescents exposed to high levels of pornography have lower levels of sexual self-esteem.
>
> Pornography use increases the marital infidelity rate by more than 300%.
>
> 56% of divorces involve one party having an "obsessive interest" in pornographic websites.

(Above statistics were from www.webroot.com/
us/en/home/resources/tips/digital-family-
life/internet-pornography-by-the-numbers)

In the article "Internet Porn: Worse Than Crack?"
(https://www.wired.com/2004/11/internet-porn-
worse-than-crack/) the dangers of pornography were
discussed. "Mary Anne Layden, co-director of the
Sexual Trauma and Psychopathology Program at the
University of Pennsylvania's Center for Cognitive
Therapy, called porn the 'most concerning thing to
psychological health that I know of existing today.'

'The internet is a perfect drug delivery system because
you are anonymous, aroused and have role models for
these behaviors,' Layden said. 'To have drugs pumped
into your house 24/7, free, and children know how to
use it better than grown-ups know how to use it – it's
a perfect delivery system if we want to have a whole
generation of young addicts who will never have the
drug out of their mind.'

"Pornography addicts have a more difficult time
recovering from their addiction than cocaine addicts,
since coke users can get the drug out of their system,
but pornographic images stay in the brain forever,"
Layden said.

Those who frequently consume Internet pornography
are less likely to marry because they see pornography
as a marital sexual gratification substitute. Malcolm,
M. & Naufal, G. (2014) "Are Pornography and
Marriage Substitutes for Young Men?" *Institute for the
Study of Labor*

Researchers believe that pornography's intense
stimulation of the brain brings about significant
changes to the brain similar to drug addiction. Simone
Kühn, Jürgen Gallinat, "Brain Structure and

Functional Connectivity Associated With Pornography Consumption: The Brain on Porn," JAMA Psychiatry 71 (July 2014): 827-834.

Consumers might tell themselves that they aren't personally affected by porn, that they won't be fooled into believing its underlying messages, but studies suggest otherwise. There is clear evidence that porn makes many consumers more likely to support violence against women, to believe that women secretly enjoy being raped, and to actually be sexually aggressive in real life. (How Consuming Porn Can Lead to Violence. Fight the New Drug)

Men who view pornography are more likely to show an increased behavioral intent to rape and are more likely to believe rape myths. Foubert, JD; Brosi MW; Bannon, RS. "Pornography Viewing amoung Fraternity Men: Effects on Bystander Intervention, Rape Myth Acceptance and Behavioral Intent to Commit Sexual Assult," *Sexual Addiction & Compulsivity*, 2011; 18(4): 212-231, at http://www.tandfonline.com/doi/abs/10.1080/10 720162.2011.625552#.VLGJH2sfrtQ

The more pornography a man watches, the more he needs to conjure images of pornography to maintain arousal and will be more likely to ask for particular sexual acts with his partner and have concerns over his sexual performance and body image. Sun. A., Bridges, A., Johnson, J. & Ezzell, M. (2014) "Pornography and the Male Sexual Script: An Analysis of Consumption and Sexual Relations." *Archives of Sexual Behavior.*

That's just the effect that porn has on the users. This doesn't account for the stories of violence, abuse, coercion, forced drug addiction and more among porn stars themselves. It is sickening to say the least.

Some women share stories of faking orgasms during a video shoot only to turn around and be vomiting in the corner the next. If they refuse to do certain scenes, positions, or scenarios, they would be forced into it or get reduced pay. The stories are too gruesome to print in this book, yet they are real.

Just spend thirty minutes on websites like fightthenewdrug.org, enough.org, or xxxChurch.com, and you will not be able to avoid the overwhelming scientific evidence that pornography is more than just a big deal. It's destroying our lives.

Wives, porn is *not* an acceptable substitute for your husband to be sexually fulfilled. Men, the woman you are masturbating to while looking at her image is *not* your wife. You are training yourself to be satisfied by a woman your wife, or future wife, cannot compete with. It's impossible to compete with a fantasy and it's irreversible what you're doing to your mind.

The scientific evidence and the sociological outcomes of pornography are irrefutable. I only shared a fraction of the information that is out there. It's alarming to say the least. Terrifying quite frankly. If you are caught in a pornography addiction, you need to seek help. Tell someone you trust. Go to one of those websites I mentioned above. There is freedom and there is an escape!

2. Is masturbation a sin?

You won't find a Bible verse that says explicitly, "masturbation is a sin," I'll give you that. What you will find is Jesus saying, "looking at a woman with lust," is a sin, and Paul says, "I must not be mastered by anything." We see the root word of "master" in the word itself, "masturbate".

I guess you could make an argument that it is possible for someone to masturbate without lusting, but I've yet to discover where that's the case. Even then, through masturbation we are seeking sexual fulfillment from someone who is not our spouse...MYSELF! I know there is disagreement on this among Christians, but when it comes to my life, I believe masturbation is a sin and should be avoided.

More often than not, masturbation is accompanied by lust, and often that lust has been created through pornography.

> Jeffrey Satinover, a psychiatrist, said this: "Pornography really does, unlike other addictions, biologically cause a direct release of the most perfect addictive substance, that is, it causes masturbation, which causes release of the naturally occurring opioids. It does what heroin cannot do." (https://www.wired.com/2004/11/internet-porn-worse-than-crack/)

> While attending a pastor's conference, I was fascinated by information that Doug Weiss, who leads the Heart To Heart Counseling Center, said about sex. During a sexual orgasm, whether through intercourse, oral sex, or masturbation, the highest level of prolactin, endorphins and other chemicals are released into the excitement center of the brain, the pre-frontal cortex. These chemicals seal the image, experience, or person into the brain and cause you to want to do it again.

> During orgasm, prolactin is released into the body. This creates the feeling of sexual satisfaction. During intercourse, four times as much prolactin is released than during masturbation. This is why the more you masturbate, the more you want or need to masturbate, because the body is not receiving the proper distribution for a sexual experience.

> During orgasm, Oxytocin is released. This is an emotional bonding agent between those involved in the sexual encounter. So, when people have multiple sex partners, they can begin to de-value attachment to a single person and move from relationship to relationship or encounter to encounter more easily. The more tolerance you develop to these chemicals,

the more pornography, sexual encounters or masturbation it requires to be satisfied.

It's a scientific fact that the more you masturbate the more semen is produced. The more semen that is produced the more your body has a desire to release it, so the more you masturbate. Which means if you masturbate, it will most likely *not* cure your problem with lust or pornography but will create a deeper one.

Is masturbation a sin? At the very least, if you are lusting during the process, absolutely. If you are "mastered" by it, finding yourself needing to masturbate or habitually doing it again, then yes! Outside of that, I think you can see the dangers of masturbation just from a scientific aspect. Masturbation is not meant to be the place we are satisfied sexually. It is not part of God's design.

As for me, I will not, and I do not masturbate. I don't want anyone satisfying me sexually other than my wife, including myself. I have made a commitment to her and a commitment to God, that masturbation will not be a part of my life, and it's not! That wasn't always the case, but for over a decade now, this has been true.

I know some men will say, "Well, I think about my spouse when I do it." Ok, what were you thinking? Were you picturing her how she looked when you dated, or how she looks now? Did you imagine her with the same breast size, stretch marks, belly flab, and body shape? Were you imagining her doing things with you that you know she'd never do, or having sex in places or positions she would never have sex? It's a slippery slope, thin ice, and I'm not willing to go there.

On the issue of porn and masturbation, I've heard many single guys say, "Well, it's only until I get married. Once I'm married it won't be a problem because then I'll have sex whenever I want." You can't hear it, but all the married men are laughing!

Listen, whatever sexual sin or addiction you have now, you are taking with you into your marriage. Marriage doesn't stop sexual sin, in fact, I think marriage is often times fuel for it!

3. What about living together before marriage?

Is it wrong to live together before you're married? According to Jesus it appeared to be, or at least He alluded to it being wrong. In John chapter 4, Jesus talks with the woman at the well. In the conversation He asks her to go get her husband. She acknowledged she didn't have one, to which Jesus said, "Your right. You've had five husbands and the man you're *living with now* is not even your husband." He didn't say, "The man you're having sex with now," but "The man you're living with now." Apparently, for Jesus, her living with someone who was not her husband was a problem.

Let's throw that aside though. I think, instead of asking the question, "Is it wrong?" we need to start asking the question, "Is it wise?" Is it wise to live together before you're married?

Well, will sexual temptation go up or down living in the same house? Up. If you're a Christian, how will this appear to people in your life who aren't Christians? Is this a positive witness or a poor one? Poor. Is this living a life that's above reproach, avoiding even the appearance of evil?

"Well, we aren't having sex," some would say. Okay. If my wife was out of town, would it be ok if I called her up and said, "Hey honey. I know you're out of town, so I'm having another woman coming over to stay the night in our house. We won't do anything physically, but she's going to sleep in our bed with me. Are you ok with that?" Absolutely not. Then why, if as singles we're supposed to keep the marriage bed pure, would that be ok before marriage?

Living together is not a trial run for marriage, it is actually training ground for divorce. Here are some numbers to look at:

> Couples who live together are 33% more likely to get divorced (sometime) after they get married. (https://contemporaryfamilies.org/cohabitation-divorce-brief-report/)

A couple who does *not* live together prior to getting married has a 20 percent chance of being divorced within five years. If the couple *has* lived together beforehand, that number jumps to 49 percent. (http://divorce.lovetoknow.com/Divorce_Statistics_and_Living_Together)

More than eight out of ten couples who live together will break up either before the wedding or afterwards in divorce.

Only 12 percent of couples who have begun their relationship with cohabitation end up with a marriage lasting 10 years or more.

Children of cohabiting parents are ten times more likely to be sexually abused by a stepparent than by a parent.

Children of cohabiting parents are three times as likely to be expelled from school or to get pregnant as teenagers than children from an intact home with married parents.

Children of cohabiting parents are five times more apt to live in poverty, and 22 times more likely to incarcerated. (http://www.rayfowler.org/2008/04/18/statistics-on-living-together-before-marriage/)

Just over 50% of first cohabiting couples ever get married.

Cohabiting couples had a separation rate five times that of married couples and a reconciliation rate that was one-third that of married couples.

Compared to those planning to marry, those cohabiting have an overall poorer relationship quality.

They tend to have more fighting and violence and less reported happiness.

Cohabiting couples earn less money and are less wealthy than their married peers later in life.

Compared to married individuals, those cohabiting have higher levels of depression and substance abuse. (https://www.thespruce.com/cohabitation-facts-and-statistics-2302236)

The science is there. You may not be able to prove that it's wrong, but you can certainly see how it isn't wise. Marriage is hard enough already without stacking the odds of success against you. Couples who live together often slide into marriage instead of deciding to get married. There is a big difference. Living together is not a trial run for marriage, it is a training ground for divorce.

4. Why should I wait to have sex?

A study done by the American Psychology Association of over 2,000 couples revealed that regardless of religious belief, couples who waited until marriage to have sex enjoyed significantly more benefits than those who chose not to wait. Among those who waited, relational stability was 22% higher, relationship satisfaction was 20% higher, sexual quality of the relationship was 15% higher and communication was 12% higher. The research said, "There's more to a relationship than sex, but we did find that those who waited longer were happier with the sexual aspect of their relationship," Busby added. "I think it's because they've learned to talk and have the skills to work with issues that come up." (https://www.sciencedaily.com/releases/2010/12/10 1222112102.htm)

"Couples who hit the honeymoon too early -- that is, prioritize sex promptly at the outset of a relationship -

> - often find their relationships underdeveloped when it comes to the qualities that make relationships stable and spouses reliable and trustworthy," said Regnerus, author of Premarital Sex in America, a book forthcoming from Oxford University Press. (https://www.sciencedaily.com/releases/2010/12/10 1222112102.htm)

Pre-marital sex destroys good relationships and prolongs bad ones. They mask other issues. Sex is like pouring fuel on a flickering flame. It ignites for a moment, but then it's gone. I heard one marriage counselor say that a large percentage of couples who end up getting divorced would never have made it to the altar were it not for pre-marital sex. The excitement, energy, and passion of sex hid other issues that were lying under the surface.

"Well, how do we know if we're compatible?" Really? Last I checked, every male and female are sexually compatible. It's how God made us!

"Well, you wouldn't buy a car without test driving it would you?" No, I wouldn't, but I also don't keep a car for a lifetime. What do I do with a car after it gets old? I trade it in. I'm not going to treat my wife, or sex, like buying a car.

So often we focus on the sex part of our relationship so much that we don't work on the non-sexual aspects. We're wanting to be compatible in bed where we spend the least amount of time together in life. Follow me for a moment.

After reading a bunch of different surveys and research, the number is not an exact science, but it's safe to say that the average sexual encounter between two people lasts about 5 minutes. Apparently, one study of over 500 couples showed experiences ranging from 33 seconds to 44 minutes. The median average being 5.4 minutes.

> "A 40-year study that surveyed more than 30,000 Americans, found in 2015 that couples who have sex once a week are the happiest."

(https://www.usatoday.com/story/news/nation-now/2017/02/09/how-often-should-you-have-sex-your-partner-sex-therapy-counseling/97545366/)

So, let's be generous and say that a couple has sex two times a week for five minutes each. That leaves 10,060 minutes left in the week where you are not having sex. Even for the couples who last 44 minutes, that's a fraction of the time we actually spend together in a marriage. I'm just saying, if we're worried about being compatible, let's actually focus on being compatible in areas that eat up more than 10 minutes of our week.

My wife and I did not have sex before marriage. I've never been with someone else nor has she. That means we have no one to compare each other to. She's the best sex I've ever had and I'm the best sex she's ever had. I could be horrible in bed and she would have no idea. I like it that way! Sex for us is the ultimate expression of love and intimacy. Sex is not love, nor is sex intimacy, but it's an expression of it.

Pornography, masturbation, cohabitation and pre-marital sex are not only discouraged from a spiritual standpoint, but from a physical, psychological, sociological and scientific one as well. You must decide what you're going to do with the evidence.

APPENDIX 2

MY GUARDRAILS

Hello, my name is Jeff Maness and I am an addict! My drug of choice? Pornography, and the lust it produces. All men have their weaknesses, mine is/was sexual sin. I know how deep that rabbit hole goes. It is dark, it is deep, and it is all consuming. Praise God, I've been sober for over 12 years and I never want to go back. For me, guardrails are a necessity.

I understand the power of one choice. When I think about the damage I could do to my marriage, my relationship with my kids, the Church I lead, and the heart of God, I am determined to live in purity. Because I know how quickly my heart can turn toward sexual sin, I have decided to put in place some guardrails to keep me safe.

Today I feel stronger and more determined than ever in my pursuit of purity. I imagine, like an alcoholic or drug addict, with every day of freedom comes a deeper and stronger faith as well. I don't have these guardrails because I'm afraid I'll fall, I have them because I acknowledge the very real possibility of falling!

None of us are immune from sin. Sin does not discriminate. It lurks around every corner. Because of that, here are the guardrails I have in place to help keep me on the path of purity. They are in no certain order.

1. **I will never be alone with another woman in private who is not my wife ---** In my ministry, I do not counsel women or meet with women alone, *ever!* On the occasions where I do need to meet with a woman, I choose to do so in our public café or in a room with the door open or window to see in. Whenever I'm meeting with a woman, I always make sure someone else knows where I am and who I'm with. Not only do I want to avoid any temptation, but I also want to avoid even the appearance of impropriety. I don't ever want there

to be a question about my motives or purity with other women.

2. **I don't travel alone** --- I've turned down speaking opportunities where the requesting organization is not able to bring my wife or accountability traveler with me. It's a part of our Church policy that we don't travel alone. We include resources in our budget for staff to travel with someone on all ministry trips. (We recently added a layer to our travel policy where we will travel in three's. "A cord of three strands is not easily broken." Ecclesiastes 4:12)

Some people ask, "Doesn't this cost a lot of money?" My response has always been, "How much is protecting our purity worth?" When we travel as a ministry, we don't let anyone stay alone in a room. When numbers are odd, we always make sure we have adjoining rooms with the door kept unlocked, or another staff member of the same sex gets a key to the room for accountability.

3. **I have weekly accountability questions asked of me** --- All our staff are held to strict accountability. Each person on our staff, me included, has an accountability partner they meet with each week and are asked specific questions. Over the years these questions have changed, here is the current list of questions I am asked each week:

A. Have you been regularly spending time in God's Word this week? Where are you currently reading?

The "where" question is great because someone who is truly reading the Word will remember where they are reading! We ask this question of potential hires as well. It has kept people from getting hired in our Church. One person confidently answered they were reading in, "Philippians 16". You should look it up!

B. Have you been regularly spending time in prayer this week?

C. **Have you exposed your mind or body to sexually inappropriate things?**

This question used to be, "Have you masturbated this week?" And yes, everyone on staff was asked this question. We changed it to a broader, more inclusive question about sexuality. I'm quick to share even the things I didn't intentionally pursue but the bait that the enemy tries to trip me up with. (ie. The thumbnails on online ads, social media posts that lure you in, etc.) Even though I don't take the bait I want everything out in the open and in the light. Sin and temptation are strongest in the dark, expose it!

D. **Have you been above reproach with your private life, finances, family, entertainment, etc.?**

E. **Have you been taking care of your body?**

F. **Is there anything you haven't told someone that you need to?**

This question gives freedom to be honest about how you're really doing. These questions aren't meant to prod they are meant to protect. I've told our staff many times, "I care more about how you're doing than what you're doing in the ministry."

G. **Have you just lied?**

We added this question just to give one final chance for honesty if needed. You might be thinking, "Couldn't people just lie with all these?" The answer is yes, but that's where we are trusting the Holy Spirit to do His job. All we can do is ask the question. If they lie, the Holy Spirit will convict them and then they have a choice to come clean.

4. **Internet accountability software** --- My computer is enabled with the Covenant Eyes accountability software. Covenant Eyes tracks all my online movement and sends a report to my accountability partner at Church, our Executive Pastor.

   What I love about Covenant Eyes is you can't access the internet without Covenant Eyes enabled. If you aren't signed in, you can't go anywhere online. If you un-install the program your accountability partner is immediately notified.

   Covenant Eyes does have a monthly fee, but it is well worth the fee. Again, what is the cost of purity? There are other free accountability programs out there as well, but Covenant Eyes has been the best for us. All staff computers at our Church are enabled with this. We personally have our entire family signed up as well.

5. **Transparency** --- Not everyone should know everything about you, but someone should. I think everyone needs someone in their life, not their spouse, that they can be completely transparent with, without fear of judgment. These people are hard to find. They are true confidants and friends. Someone who, no matter what you share with them, is held in complete confidence and without condemnation.

   This person should be someone not directly affected by any choice that you make (ie. employee, employer, immediate family, etc.) My confidant is Todd. I can tell him anything (and have), and I know the information is safe and I know he's got my back. Whether it's a private, deep conversation about my past, or the text saying "I'm being tempted. Please pray," I know that my soul is safe with him.

   Again, sin and temptation are most powerful in the dark. Just having someone to bring temptation into the light with is so re-assuring.

What are your guardrails? Do you have any? They don't have to be the same as mine. These are what help me the most. Where do you need help? I encourage you to sit down, pray about it, and put the guardrails in place that you need to keep you aggressive at purity.

APPENDIX 3

MY GAME-PLAN FOR PURITY

Everyone needs a game-plan against sin. Your game-plan doesn't have to look the same as mine, but you need a game-plan. Game-plans don't guarantee victory, but they sure help. I've yet to hear of a championship team or individual that rose to the top without a game-plan. Even in sports like golf, where it's you against the course, a game-plan is necessary to win.

Aggression is what we are after. Aggression against sin. Typically, the most aggressive teams in sports are the ones with the clearest game-plan. A game-plan takes the thinking out of the situation. When "this" happens, I'm going to do "this."

It took me years to master my game-plan. I've added to the list and I've taken things away, but 12 years into my life of purity and these are my go-to things. These aren't things I do in any particular order they are just all a part of my game-plan. Like the guardrails, I encourage you to develop your own game-plan to defeat whatever area of sin you find yourself the weakest.

1. Play worship music as much as possible --- I'm not against other music, I'm just partial to worship music in my life. Worship is warfare! I can't think of anything else that attacks the enemy like worship does. Yes, I can pray, and I do, but it's worship that gets me seeking Jesus the fastest and slaying temptation the most.

One of my favorite verses in the Bible is 2 Chronicles 20:22. By itself it wouldn't make much sense, but within the context of the story it is incredibly powerful.

Israel was facing the imposing armies of Amon, Moab and Mount Seir. King Jehoshaphat and the people of Israel were terrified by what they faced, and they begged God for help.

God commands the people to go out the next day and face the armies that were bearing down on them, but he told them something odd. "Put the worshipers out front." Seriously, you should read the whole story.

So, very early the next morning the army of Israel goes out to face certain doom while the worship team was out front to get slaughtered. They set out, singing praises to the Lord, and look what happens:

2 Chronicles 20:22 - At the very moment they began to sing and give praise, the Lord caused the armies of Ammon, Moab and Mount Seir to start fighting among themselves.

When the army of Judah arrived at the battlefield all they saw were the dead bodies of their enemy. Their worship had waged warfare on their behalf.

Now, I'm not saying that if you play worship music you'll never be tempted again in your life. I just believe that the more we send worship out ahead of us, the more the enemy is attacked for us in our lives. And besides, is more worship ever a bad thing in our lives? For this reason and more, I choose to play worship music more than anything else in my life.

2. Say "No" out loud to the enemy --- Like I talked about in chapters four and five, we don't need to find impurity, it finds us. If you're anything like me (and most guys are), you can be tempted at the most random of places. Anytime and anywhere that our minds are open to wander, the enemy will leap in.

Let me be clear, temptation is *not* sin. When an image flashes in your mind, you aren't accountable for the flash but for the follow through. When an attractive woman crosses your path, you aren't accountable for seeing, you're accountable for seeking her with your eyes and mind. It's not the initial thought that is the sin, it's the capturing of that thought, and second (or third) look that leads to sin.

For me, what I've found super helpful in combating the temptation to chase those thoughts is saying, "No!", out loud. When I'm alone, I'll say it emphatically. There are times when this would be super weird, so I say it underneath my breath or even in my head. Consciously saying "No!" seems to reset the brain and recalibrate my heart. It reminds me what I'm ultimately after, I'm after the Lord!

I believe, on the humanity side of Jesus He even did this. In this particular scene, it wasn't a sexual temptation, but a moment where Christ could have "given in". In that moment, He spoke out loud to his flesh. As Jesus was inching closer and closer to his crucifixion, He uttered these words:

John 18:27-28 [27] "Now my soul is deeply troubled. Should I pray, 'Father, save me from this hour'? But this is the very reason I came! [28] Father, bring glory to your name."

I believe Jesus was being tempted to throw in the towel. To give it up! We know from His prayer in the garden that He did not want to face the cross. He asked the Father for any other way. Call me a heretic, but in this moment, I think the humanity of Jesus was overwhelmed and He was tempted to call in the cavalry. To give up. But He didn't. He audibly reminded Himself of the reason He came, "Father, bring glory to Your name."

When we say, "No!" we are audibly reminding ourselves of what we're after. We are here to bring glory to the Lord. If I give in to this thought or this action, I will be going against the very reason I exist. "Father, bring glory to Your name!" Say, "NO!"

Sometimes one "No!" isn't good enough. The devil doesn't give up that easily. At times, I have literally had shouting matches with the enemy when it seems like a barrage of impure thoughts are flooding my mind. I've said, "No, no, no, no, NO!" on many occasions. I would hope that if a woman physically propositioned me I would emphatically say, "NO!", as well. So why would I not treat the devil the same way in my mind?

3. Say "Jesus" out loud --- How many songs have been written about the power of the name of Jesus? I could rattle off a handful of songs right now that speak of the power in His name. It's at the name of Jesus that every knee will bow, and every tongue confess. (Philippians 2:10-11) It was the name of Jesus that the demons in Acts chapter 19 said they knew and obeyed. There is power in the name of Jesus.

If Jesus is the name that holds power over the enemy, I speak it out loud whenever I can. When "No" doesn't do the trick, "Jesus" typically does.

I'm going to be blunt here, but I say this to guys all the time. It's awfully difficult to masturbate when you're saying the name of Jesus out loud. Apply that to any sin. It's more difficult to make that extra click on the computer, dwell on that channel or go one base further, when you're saying the name of Jesus out loud.

Again, sometimes I have to do this under my breath or in my head, but when I say Jesus' name He moves on my behalf.

4. Change of place --- When possible, I will try and change my physical location when I'm tempted. I've walked outside, left the room, found another room with people in it, whatever it takes to get out of the place where the temptation is. If I'm being tempted on my phone I need to set it down and walk away. If it's the TV, the computer, even inside of a movie theater, am I willing to walk out so I'll be able to stand up against sin? Sometimes, all you need to escape temptation is to change the place you are in.

5. Tell someone you're struggling --- Sin grows in darkness. When we bring temptation to light it begins to lose its power. Sometimes, just a text to someone, or a quick phone call can alleviate the temptation you're under. Do you have this person in your life? If not, who could it be? Everyone needs someone!

As I've shared, my person is Todd. With a quick text, I can not only let someone know that I'm being attacked, but I have a prayer warrior lifting me up as well.

None of these things will stop temptation, but they will give you strength against it. Obviously, we need the power of the Holy Spirit in our lives to set us free. But as I said in chapter four, the power of God without the right practices in our life is pointless.

APPENDIX 4

THE WIFE'S PURPOSE

In Chapter 7 – Part 1, we talked almost exclusively about the purpose or role of the husband in marriage. This is a book written for men, but I understand and hope that many women will read this as well. So, it would not be fair nor prudent, if I did not address the wife's role here.

I know there is lots of stigma attached to the phrase, "role of the wife." That conjures up images of a 1950's mentality where the woman's "role" was to be barefoot, pregnant, and in the kitchen. When I use the word "role" that is in no way what I'm talking about.

As the father of three daughters, and the husband of a woman who has an entrepreneurial spirit, I am all for women being all God designed them to be and pursuing anything He calls them to do.

I want to see barriers lifted for my daughters to excel in whatever field they find themselves in. So, this is not an expression of what I believe women should do with their lives. These are principles, that regardless of what you do for a living should guide your love in marriage.

I truly do believe, if the husband lived out his role first, then most women would have no problem living in theirs. Yes, there will always be disagreements and speed bumps, and no, it will not be easy. Here in Ephesians 5, God through the Apostle Paul lays out the roles of a husband and wife.

Ephesians 5:22-23 **[22] For wives, this means submit to your husbands as to the Lord. [23] For a husband is the head of his wife as Christ is the head of the Church. He is the Savior of his body, the Church.**

Remember, both the husband and wife are to submit to one another out of reverence for Christ. Jesus should be our first pursuit and submission should be our first priority.

So, in the same way I asked the men in Chapter 7, "How did Jesus love us?" We also need to ask the women, "How do we submit to Christ?" That is the description Paul uses. "Submit to your husbands *as to* the Lord."

This one is trickier to me. For one, I'm speaking as a man to women, and I recognize that. Two, the examples of how Christ loved us are much clearer than examples of submission. It's one thing to challenge men to love their wives as Christ loved the Church. Who's going to argue with the value of seeking, serving and spoiling someone you love? But submission? That's no easy task to communicate or pursue.

Ladies, just as there are more than three ways we men should love you in marriage, there are more than three ways that you can submit. But I'm going to present three things a wife can do every day that will help her submit to her husband.

Respect your husband

In Ephesians 5, at the end of Paul's discourse on marriage, he sums up his teaching here:

Ephesians 5:33 - So again I say, each man must love his wife as he loves himself, and the wife must respect her husband.

That word "Respect" means, "To entertain a high esteem for him, being desirous of pleasing him in all things lawful, reasonable and proper. Honor."

Ladies, I understand, I really do, how frustrating it can be to live with us men. There are many times we don't do what you think we should do, focus where you want us to focus, or live how you want us to live, and most of the time you're probably right. Many times, it's because we haven't taken responsibility, so it feels like you must lead the home, and in your effort to lead, we feel disrespected.

Deep down, I believe every man is dying to take responsibility in their marriage and they are desperate for respect. They either don't lead because they're afraid to fail, or they can't because their wife won't let them. The greatest respect you can show your husband is to let him lead, even if you disagree!

This doesn't mean you become a doormat, or that you never speak your mind. It means you, "entertain a high esteem for him, being desirous of pleasing him in all things lawful, reasonable and proper. Honor."

Rejoice with your husband

Psalm 40:16 - But may all who search for you be filled with joy and gladness in you. May those who love your salvation repeatedly shout, "The LORD is great!"

Lift your husband up verbally. Encourage him. Support him. Be his biggest fan. Let him know how much you appreciate him and all he does for the family. Even when he's not doing everything you think he should, rejoice with him that he's your man!

I have never met a man who disagreed with me on this: After Jesus, the opinion that matters most to us is our wives'. I love it when someone tells me how great my sermon was or how much it meant to them, but there is nothing like walking off the platform and seeing a text from my wife rejoicing with me. "AWESOME message! I love it when you preach on this subject."

There is a text waiting for me almost every week when I walk off the stage. Not only will Sabrina encourage me, but she'll let me know how it applied to her life. That's a game changer in our marriage. My wife is for me, and she doesn't let me forget it.

Your husband needs to know not only do you respect him, but you believe in him as well. Sometimes you might have to think really long and hard about what you could rejoice with him about but find something. Start to encourage him about the things he's good at and he'll start doing better at the things he's not.

Relate to your husbands

James 4:8 - Come close to God, and God will come close to you.

This one is perhaps the hardest. When I think about how we submit to Christ and then compare that to marriage, it gets deep really quick! When we submit to Christ we take on His plans, dreams, ambitions, and desires. I know this sounds sexist but hear me out. I promise you it is not.

When you submit to your husband, you take on his plans, dreams, ambitions, and desires as well. This does not mean you negate or neglect your own, and it doesn't mean that he gets to ignore yours. It simply means that you are aligning yourself with your husband.

I was talking with one of the pastors on our staff about this concept once and he said, "That's exactly what my wife did for me." I said, "Explain!" He replied, "When God called me to leave the job I had with the government and become a pastor at the Church, my wife said, 'I'm all in.'" That's it!

I've heard my mom and wife say this before as well to my dad and I: "God called me to you first. I am your wife. So, wherever God calls you, He's calling me as well. I'm with you."

"I will honor you, I'm for you, I'm with you." Ladies, that sums up submission pretty well. Respect, rejoice with, and relate to your husband. Draw near to him (your husband), and he will draw near to you! Take on and participate in his plans, dreams, ambitions, and desires! Assume every day that he's not sure you're still "with" him, and then set out that day to prove to him that you are.

Can you imagine what would happen in our homes if the men started to seek, serve, and spoil their wives every day, and women began to respect, rejoice with, and relate to their husbands? We would see a revolution in our homes that this world has never seen before.

NOTES

Chapter 3: Bold Faith
1. Luke Tyerman, *The Life and Times of the Rev. John Wesley* (London, 1871), III:632.

Chapter 4 – Aggressive at Purity
1. John C. Maxwell, *The 21 Indispensable qualities of a leader.* (Nashville, TN: Thomas Nelson, 1999), xi.
2. The word Echad. Gill's Exposition of the Entire Bible, Genesis 2:24. Christianity.com online source. https://www.christianity.com/bible/commentary.php?com=gill&b=1&c=2

Chapter 5 – A Game-Plan For Purity
1. "Steve Irwin - Biography." *The Internet Movie Database (IMDb)*, www.imdb.com/name/nm0410455/bio?ref_=nm_ov_bio_sm.

Chapter 6 – Taking responsibility
1. Bennett, William J. "Why Men Are in Trouble - CNN.com." *CNN.com - Breaking News, U.S., World, Weather, Entertainment & Video News*, www.cnn.com/2011/10/04/opinion/bennett-men-in-trouble/index.html?iref=allsearch.

Chapter 7 Part 1 --- Taking Responsibility In My Marriage
1. "The 5 Love Languages™ | Five Love Languages." *Home - Five Love Languages*, www.5lovelanguages.com/learn-the-languages/the-five-love-languages/.
2. Meaning of the word "Submit": Strong, James (1890), *The Exhaustive Concordance of the Bible*, (Cincinnati: Jennings & Graham. 1890)

Chapter 7 Part 2 --- Taking Responsibility In My Parenting
1. "Carrie Underwood, Jesus, Take The Wheel Lyrics." *Country Lyrics, Tabs, Chords @ Cowboy Lyrics, Music*, www.cowboylyrics.com/lyrics/underwood-carrie/jesus-take-the-wheel-16549.html.

Chapter 8 – Honor God Financially
1. Sangl, Joseph, "I Was Broke, Now I'm Not" (United States of America: www.morrispublishing.com, 2007) www.iwbnin.com.

Chapter 9 – Live For Eternity
1. "YouTube - Michael Jordan 'Be Like Mike' (Originally aired 1992) Gatorade Commercial." *YouTube - Broadcast Yourself.*, www.youtube.com/watch?v=06dQSwnxBbM.
2. "MICHAEL JORDAN, COME FLY WITH ME." *YouTube*, YouTube, 3 Jan. 2015, www.youtube.com/watch?v=qdNF2NUVL9w.
3. "Quote: Only One Life, Twill Soon Be Past – Poem by C.T Studd." *Paul Hockley*, 21 Feb. 2017, paulhockley.com/2016/05/24/quote-only-one-life-twill-

Chapter 10 – Lead Courageously
1. Seitz, M. (2017). *Hacksaw Ridge Movie Review & Film Summary (2016) | Roger Ebert.* [online] Rogerebert.com. Available at: http://www.rogerebert.com/reviews/hacksaw-ridge-2016.
2. Meaning of "Be Courageous": Strong, James (1890), *The Exhaustive Concordance of the Bible*, (Cincinnati: Jennings & Graham. 1890)

Chapter 11 – Leave A Legacy
1. Mark Batterson, *In A Pit With A Lion On A Snowy Day: How to survive and thrive when opportunity roars.* (United States of America: Multnomah, 2016 First Revised Edition)
2. *Gladiator.* (2000). [film] Universal Pictures: Ridley Scott.
3. *Braveheart*, directed by Mel Gibson (1995; Hollywood: Paramount Home Video, 2002), DVD.
4. *300, directed by Zach Snyder.* (2006). DVD

Chapter 12 – Who's Your Hushai
1. "Intimacy": *New Oxford American Dictionary, 2nd edition.* NY: Oxford U. Press. 2005 - Apple Dictionary on Macbook Pro

About The Author:

Jeff Maness is the founding and Lead Pastor of Element Church in Cheyenne, WY, and the author of the book *"Because You're Called: Three Words That Will Change Your Life"* and *"The Christmas Cloth."*

His first calling is to his family. He married his high school sweetheart (Sabrina) in June of 1997, and they saw their family grow from two to six in the first 9 years of their marriage. They have one son (Jonah), and three daughters (Mariah, Makalah and Jaydah).

He and Sabrina take very seriously the call to raise their children according to God's will! Jeff says, "If you're not careful, you can be so moved, so inspired, so 'called' by God that you'll end up pursuing *it* at the cost of your family."

In December 1997, Jeff graduated from Oklahoma Wesleyan University with a degree in Pastoral Ministry. He immediately began pastoring a little country Church in Ringwood, OK before God led he and Sabrina to Gillette, WY to serve in youth ministry. In February 2006, God would place a clear calling on Jeff's heart to start Element Church in Cheyenne, WY.

The vision of Element Church is to guide people to experience life to its fullest, connect them into meaningful relationships and help them make a lasting impact! What began with six people in the basement of the Maness home has turned into a movement of people living out that vision in whatever community God has placed them.

To contact Jeff for speaking at an event or coaching availability, please email him at hello@jeffmaness.com. Follow Jeff on Twitter, Instagram or Facebook: jeffgmaness

To learn more about Element Church and what God is doing through their ministry, please visit www.elementChurch.life

TODAY, our world is in desperate need of men. Not men in quantity, but men in character. **"My Declaration"** is written as a challenge for men to rise-up and live in that character through their God given purpose and potential in this life. Something was started within us as men when we were born. Something was placed in us by God Himself that lies dormant and ready to rise. Through this book you will be challenged to rise-up with a bold faith and finish what was started in you by being aggressive at purity, taking responsibility, honoring God financially, leading courageously, and leaving a legacy. Those things are already at the core of every man, we just need to rise-up and live them out as men. This is My Declaration! It can be yours as well.

I am proud to call Jeff my Brother. And, I am equally proud of this book and its possible impact in your life. I hope this book challenges you like never before. I hope this book disturbs you to act and do the work of being a man. I hope this book prompts you to get after all four areas of your life (God, relationships, profession, body). I hope you start to see that the King of Kings is calling you to expand like never before.

BRYAN MILES | CEO AND FOUNDER OF BELAY SOLUTIONS

JEFF MANESS

is the founding and Lead Pastor of Element Church in Cheyenne, WY. He is the author of "Because You're Called: Three Words That Will Change Your Life," and "21: A 21-Day Journey For The New Believer."

To learn more about Jeff, his books, or his leadership you can visit **WWW.JEFFMANESS.COM.**

$15.00
ISBN 978-0-692-16892-9

9 780692 168929
51500>